Practical business planning

# Practical business planning

John Chandler
*Director of Planning*
*Reed International PLC*

Published in association with
The Institute of Chartered Accountants
in England and Wales

## McGRAW-HILL BOOK COMPANY

**London** · New York · St Louis · San Francisco · Auckland
Bogotá · Guatemala · Hamburg · Lisbon · Madrid · Mexico
Montreal · New Delhi · Panama · Paris · San Juan
São Paulo · Singapore · Sydney · Tokyo · Toronto

Published by

McGRAW-HILL Book Company (UK) Limited
MAIDENHEAD · BERKSHIRE · ENGLAND
In association with The Institute of Chartered Accountants
in England and Wales

**British Library Cataloguing in Publication Data**
Chandler, John, 1932–
    Practical business planning.
    1. Corporate planning
    I. Title
    658.4'012      HD30.28

    ISBN 0-07-084172-1

**Library of Congress Cataloging-in-Publication Data**
Chandler, John.
    Practical business planning.
    1. Corporate planning. 2. Managerial accounting.
    I. Title.

    HD30.28.C45    1987      658.4'012      87-3240

    ISBN 0-07-084172-1

12345WL8987

Typeset by Eta Services (Typesetters) Ltd, Beccles, Suffolk
and printed and bound in Great Britain by Whitstable Litho Ltd, Whitstable, Kent

# Contents

# PART 1
# The concepts of planning

Most business people are familiar with the structure of accounts and methods of accounting. But the links between the profit and loss or balance sheet figures of the business and the markets within which it operates, or the other influences which affect it, are not always clear. How important is a big market share, what is the impact of vertical integration, what difference does high (or low) inflation make? These questions can only be answered by analysing that much wider information base which underlies the accounts and of which the periodic figures are only a snapshot summary.

Planning is about this analysis—about understanding the structure and dynamics of business. In a turbulent environment, with smart competition, it provides the road-map to competitive advantage.

This book is intended as a practical guide for those who already have some knowledge of accounting. Part 1 is concerned with concepts, offering a blueprint for thinking about business. It explains how a planning system may be built and why it should be built in such a way. This involves a view of the structure of business, the markets and competition and the environment generally in which it operates. These aspects are inserted into a framework of objectives and strategic, tactical and financial planning. Together, these separate pieces may be seen as the components of a planning machine. The final chapter of Part 1 assembles all the components into this machine. This then sets the scene for Part 2 which describes how the machine may be used most effectively in practice.

# 1

# What is planning for?

## The meaning of planning

When Jack Robinson, the manager of a small plastic pipe extrusion business operating out of a factory in North London, says that next week he is going to get stuck into his business plans, he probably has a very different idea of what he is going to be doing compared to Sir James Forbes, CB, chairman of a leading multinational corporation, with its elegant country seat in the Berkshire countryside. Their purpose at least is clear—to outsmart the competition, but the way each goes about it will be vastly different. Yet both use the words 'business planning' to describe what they are doing.

What is meant by business planning? Perhaps it is too simplistic to say that planning is merely thinking before acting.[1] It has been defined as 'the design of a desired future and of effective ways of bringing it about.'[2] There are many other ways of describing the process,[3] but this one does get closer to the roots in that it emphasizes the expected outcome. It does not, however, spell out some very important features of planning, and, in particular, that any design, to be effective, will be based upon the best information available, properly analysed, concisely and clearly communicated.

Many managers such as Jack Robinson, with limited staff, on a tight budget and pressed for time, would challenge the need for extensive analysis and prefer to work in a loose, intuitive way. Indeed at every level of corporate size, from the small independent firm to the giant multinational, the pendulum swings between this attitude and the more systematic one. Planning is as much subject to fashion as is any other human activity. At times, in the larger companies, everyone is hiring expensive consultants and experts to design and implement systems, employing armies of researchers to pore over the business, holding strategy conferences and producing dazzling blueprints for the future. At other times, business planning is in disrepute, gut feel holds sway, consultants and experts are only used on specific projects, planning staffs are cut, conferences are about the here and now, and there is no commitment on future action.

If this is so, could business get along without any sort of formal planning? Why should managers not succeed in the future as they have in the past, through experience of the market place coupled with careful control of the cash flow? It is always possible that some managers may do so—those with outstanding skills and intuition. But, in general, the increasing complexity of commercial life means that most have to use some help. The aim must be to devise a satisfactory compromise between the excesses of either the analytical or the intuitive approach.

### The benefits of planning

There is, in any event, no escaping information technology. Society builds its own treadmills and the commercial world is no exception. Having developed information techniques and the microcomputers on which to play with information, the smart operators, in their search for competitive advantage, are going to get as much value as they can out of this. The rest will ultimately have to follow suit if they are not to fall too far behind in the competitive game.

However reluctantly they may do so, they will find a very considerable benefit in a systematic approach to planning. The process of planning offers these advantages:

- learning about the realities of the business;
- focusing on critical issues;
- enabling the review of alternative futures;
- setting performance standards;
- providing guidelines to staff.

The first of these advantages arises from actually going through the formal analysis. This is a necessary preliminary to the preparation of any plans, but its main benefit is in educating those who follow through the process.

Suppose Tom Piper, one of Sir James Forbes's managers, interested in developing into further sectors of his business area, says to his chief accountant: 'I want to get into foil laminates. Will you put together a proposal for head office? I'd like to get it in by Friday week. I'll glance through it before it goes in.' This delegation of a project could be standard practice in this business. At the meeting with head office, however, it will be the chief accountant who answers all the questions and dictates the stance towards the market. In such circumstances he is acting as the chief executive, even if he does not have the title or get the pay cheque. The reality is that, while information-gathering may be delegated, planning cannot be. Managers who want to stay in charge will not leave it to their subordinates to review the information and slant the project. By participating in depth in the preparation of the plans, they gain sufficient knowledge and understanding to control what goes on.

The second benefit is that of enabling managers to focus on critical issues. With information technology advancing so fast, it is easy to become overwhelmed by the mass of data. Furthermore, the media are producing an ever-increasing deluge of unselected information which tends to be sold on the drama of its headlines rather than on the probability of its happening, or the impact were it to occur. Jack Robinson reads in the papers of the likely change in oil prices, a drop in sterling, Nigerian trade embargoes, US steel protection, EEC proposals for worker consultation and agreement on the future of Hong Kong. He wonders how it will all affect him.

Proper analysis means that managers know the sensitivity of their business to changes in the environment and they can ignore the irrelevant. Jack Robinson knows that there is a relationship between oil and polymer prices, that the former are designated in dollars and that Nigeria is a big market for his product. So he pays attention to these items. He also knows that the EEC proposals are unlikely to come forward for a long time and he cannot see how he is in any way directly affected by Hong Kong. He can ignore these items. He may be less aware of the way in which a US steel embargo may affect steel prices. Suppose he wants to move into high pressure mouldings of car bumpers and other large automotive parts. The way in which steel prices influence the competitiveness of UK motor manufacture and hence the number of plastic bumpers required becomes relevant. Once he has had a look at this problem, he will know how critical it is. Then he will know whether he will have to concern himself with this news item in the future. It will make the job a lot simpler.

Third, the techniques now available for analysing information give the manager the opportunity to delve into future uncertainty. Until modern methods of information manipulation became readily available, the only way to find out how different events would affect a business was to live through them and learn by experience. This was often a very expensive and traumatic process. Information science today permits the simulation of the real world. Jack Robinson could model the new high pressure plastic moulding market he wants to penetrate, and could try to find out how the competition might respond, what sort of price/volume balance could be sustained against what levels of market growth and so on. He would certainly be foolish to rely on the results of such simulation as a certainty, but he would be able to get a feel for how his business and his plans for it might stand up to change, particularly in areas where he has no personal experience.

Finally, any business which is more than a one-man band has to have guidelines for its staff, firstly to enable performance to be tracked and to indicate who are doing well and who badly; but also, it enables the staff to use their own experience and knowledge more effectively in helping the business to thrive. Setting guidelines does not mean the preparation of detailed sets of plans which attempt to cover any contingency, so that the individual has only to take down a manual, thumb through to page 107A and read precisely what to do. Apart from the impossibility of producing any such manual to cover every conceivable future event, it would act as a strait-jacket and would do away with the need for any creativity among members of staff. An army of robots would suffice in such a business. Unexpected events in the real world need flexible responses such as only trained and competent humans can offer. What are needed, therefore, are general signposts of strategic and tactical direction. The sales manager of the plastics factory, for example, aware that it is the intention to move out of an unprofitable line, will use his judgement, when faced with an unexpected series of price cuts by the competition, whether to introduce new lines at an earlier date than planned, or to go with the opposition, or deliberately to shed market share.

## Forecasting and budgeting

Given the advantages of planning, what does it encompass? Clearly, it includes a very wide variety of disciplines and skills. Those who equate it with forecasting alone are wrong. Forecasting plays an important part in planning, but it is far from the whole. The process may start with the salesman's forecasts, but these need to be considered in the light of:

- the competition, such study to be undertaken by the market manager—probably Robinson himself;
- inflation and growth, from economic reports;
- the availability of labour as predicted by the personnel manager;
- plant capacity from the production manager's plan;
- raw materials, as seen by the buyers.

The various members of staff have to make their own assessments of the validity of the original forecast, look at the options available and make their choice: this goes right through the hierarchy. Jack Robinson must be concerned not only with what his salesmen think they can sell, but also with how much he wants them to sell in the light of competition and his financial, labour and production resources. The important feature of planning is the way in which skilled and experienced managers and their advisers continually sift through the mass of past data and the forecasts and come to conclusions about the design for the future. This is far more than forecasting.

There are organizations that seem to take the view that budgeting is an adequate substitute for planning. Budgeting is the preparation of detailed financial targets tied to specific management actions. The budget has virtually no flexibility. It represents the tip of the planning iceberg, but unless the whole process has been gone through, with a proper assessment of all the information and an understanding of how the business will respond to unexpected events in its markets, budgeting is an empty exercise and its inflexibility will be a clog on achieving success. The business will not know how to react to change.

Planning, therefore, is not a simple forecasting or budgeting exercise. It is multi-disciplinary, and requires a lot of thought if it is going to achieve its purpose of giving an edge over the competition and of maintaining a profitable business. If, however, Jack Robinson's plastics factory is a small independent business, he is going to complain, quite rightly, that he does not have the resources to indulge in such exercises. This is a problem that can be overcome and it is addressed in Part 2 of this book.

The question considered at this point is whether there is any intrinsic difference in the way Jack Robinson and Sir James Forbes have to plan. Do differences in size and market and type of product make such a difference that there are no common features? Or can similar techniques and structures be applied to all commercial organizations in building up a systematic picture of the business?

## Planning in different types of business

It is clear that business is a very diverse sort of activity. It may be classified in a number of different ways, including:

- span of markets;
- style of management;
- level of ownership.

These all have an effect upon the way in which the chief executive officer (CEO) will look at the operations and put the strategies together.

The span of markets refers to the different sets of customers to whom the business sells. These are not just defined by the product or service offered, but also by location. The producer of a product such as gold has one market worldwide, even though it may be sold through London, New York and Tokyo. The principal buyers may deal in all these exchanges. At the other end of the market scale are products such as local newspapers. These have very narrow market places as each newspaper has virtually no sale outside its own area—mid-Hertfordshire, Dayton, Ohio, or wherever.

On another dimension of span, the organization may offer a very wide diversity of product; Reed International, the UK multi-business group, for example, in 1980 served over 70 different markets, including pulp, paper-making, packaging, paint, plastic conversion, plumbing and publishing—everything beginning with the letter 'P'! Thus market span may embrace either or both of the dimensions of location and product, and result in a highly complex organization. It is not, however, size which makes for complexity—the international commodity group may have a simpler business than the individual running a bunch of local newspapers—it is diversity which creates the problems.

The next factor, style of management, is to a very great extent influenced by the previous dimension. Thus a company may be an industrial concentrate that is vertically integrated in a limited product range. It starts with activities in raw material exploitation and goes right through the production chain down to the ultimate retail customer. Oil companies were of this nature, though more recently many have moved into a number of new development areas. BP is a UK oil giant that has been diversifying—into biochemicals, computer sciences and so on. An industrial concentrate will have a significant number of operating managers assembled at the company headquarters—and marketing, R&D and such activities will also tend to be centralized. This is not feasible in a highly diversified company which is forced to disperse to the relevant operating units not only operating management, but also many key staff functions.

Independently, however, of the degree of vertical integration, a number of business sectors, particularly in the services area, seem to demand a style of their own; for instance, retail stores and financial institutions. Such types of business will have different management structures compared to the normal manufacturing organization. A group may have a number of investments or non-wholly owned subsidiaries. These will have to be managed in a different way from an integrated set of businesses—the interests of minority share-holders preclude the full incorporation of such operations into the parent group

**Table 1.1**   Organization chart, Rio Tinto Zinc Corporation PLC

| 100% owned | less than 100% owned | % |
|---|---|---|
| | CRA (Australasia) | 52.9 |
| | Argyle Diamond Mines | 56.8 |
| RTZ Borax | Australian Mining & Smelting | |
| RTZ Chemicals | Bougainville Copper | 53.6 |
| | Comalco | 67.0 |
| RTZ Oil & Gas | Hammersley Holdings | 93.7 |
| | Blair Atholl Coal | 50.2 |
| Tunnel Holdings | Kembla Coal & Coke | |
| RTZ Cement | Tarong | |
| | Dampier Salt | 64.9 |
| Thos. W. Ward | Mary Kathleen Uranium | 52.8 |
| | Rio Algom (Canada) | 52.8 |
| | Lornex Mining Corp | 68.1 |
| Rio Tinto South Africa | | |
| | Palabora Mining Co. | 38.9 |
| | Rossing Uranium (Namibia) | 46.5 |
| RTZ Metals | | |
| Capper Pas | Duisburger Kupferhutte | 99.2 |
| Carnon Consol Tin Mines | Rio Tinto Minera | 49.0 |
| RTZ Aluminium Holdings | Geever Tin Mines | 17.9 |
| Rionfinex | South Crofty | 40.0 |
| Tinto Holdings Zimbabwe | | |
| | Rio Tinto Zimbabwe | 58.4 |
| | Brinco | 25.7 |
| | Emp de Cobre Cerro Colorado | 49.0 |

Source: Report and Accounts 1983

and in particular the movement of cash round the group. Consider, for example, an organization such as Rio Tinto Zinc Corporation which has a large number of major investments round the world, the majority of which are not wholly owned. Table 1.1 sets out the principal companies involved. The problems of such an organization have to be very different from those of a brewer in Scotland, or of a package holiday operator in the Midlands.

## The components of planning

It is, nevertheless, now a fact that certain essentials of planning are common to all these types of business, notwithstanding their diversity, their management style and their ownership structure. Over the past 20 years, a considerable body of knowledge has been built up about planning which applies irrespective of the sort of business involved.

Broadly, this shows that the components of any planning system which are both appropriate and, indeed, essential to every type of organization may be summarized as follows:

- analysis of business structure;
- statement of objectives;
- in-depth market and competitive study;
- review of economic and other environmental factors;
- development of strategies which flow from the foregoing;
- development of the tactics needed to achieve the strategies;
- financial evaluation and allocation of resources.

The following chapters of Part 1 look at these various aspects of planning in detail and describe the concepts against the real world of business. The case for planning is made from the basis of practice.

## Notes

1. R. Amara and A. J. Lipinski, *Business Planning for an Uncertain Future*, Pergamon Press, Oxford, 1983.
2. R. L. Ackoff, *A Concept of Corporate Planning*, Wiley, New York, 1970.
3. See also, generally, H. I. Ansoff, *Corporate Strategy*, McGraw-Hill, New York, 1965.

# 2

# The jargon

## Specialized languages

'Northants last-ball run to top of table', announced a headline in *The Times* of Monday, 2 September, 1985. Most English people will instantly recognize this as a comment on some cricketing event. To explain to a foreigner what it all signifies would, however, require intricate excursions into the meaning of 'ball' in this context and how many 'balls' the particular version of the game involved; what a 'run' is, and so on. To explain to the fans, however, in full and plain language on each occasion would be both tedious and unnecessary. They know the language.

In the same way, business language is specialized—and nowhere more so than in economics! Thus a stockbroking firm recently commented that 'In July, the publication of a smaller than expected merchandise deficit figure ... gave rise to speculation that the net trade component of the Q3 "flash" GNP estimate would be a positive contribution to growth for the first time since 1984 Q4.'[1] This is readily understandable by those who are economy watchers, or who are concerned with the impact of movements in trade. Again, they speak the language. For those who are not so familiar, some explanations are needed.

There is another complication, however, in that in many instances there is no fixed agreement on the way in which some terms can be applied. A word such as 'objectives' can mean anything from a short-term management action to the timeless mission of a business. In this chapter, therefore, definitions are introduced of some of the more important vocabulary, particularly where there may not be a universally accepted usage. The words explained are shown in *sloping* type. This is not intended to be a dictionary, so only a limited range is covered and, in particular, commonly used and understood accounting terms such as 'cash flow' and 'profit' are not defined. The references at the end of the chapter give guidance on sources for accounting and economics.[2]

## The planning framework

The first area tackled relates to the framework for planning, i.e. words such as 'objectives', 'strategies', and 'goals'. The term '*objective*' is taken to mean the overall reason why the business is in being. Other commentators adopt for this, words such as 'mission', 'leitbild', 'overarching goal' and so on.[3] It does not, in fact, matter what is adopted as long as the meaning is clear and it is applied consistently.

Within an objective, or set of objectives, there is a hierarchy of long-term and short-term actions. These are labelled as follows:

- *Strategy*  The means in market terms to achieve the corporate objectives (e.g. to achieve a major UK market share in plastic food containers);
- *Goal*  A specific criterion for quantifying a strategy (e.g. increase market share to 15 per cent by year 2);
- *Tactic*  The means to achieve a strategy (e.g. improve competitiveness through increased productivity on plastic food containers' line through automation);
- *Target*  A specific criterion for quantifying a tactic (e.g. reduce unit labour costs on plastic food containers by 7 per cent in year 1).

Thus, strategies and tactics both come within the overall objectives, and tactics (and indeed financial plans) cascade down from the strategies. There is no universal acceptance of this classification, but it gives a helpful framework within which the structure of the planning system can be more readily discussed.

## Markets

Strategy in the business context requires an understanding of '*market*' and the concept of market share. All business starts in 'the market place', but there are very many market places. The market has to be defined more precisely to help business people in planning what they are going to do. One definition is: 'the arena within which the price and demand for a product or service are set'.[4]

The '*market share*' of a business is the percentage share of total goods or services sold by that business in the defined market. The goods or services do not have to be identical: hyacinths may compete with garden gnomes for the amateur gardener's money. At a more sophisticated level, advertising is sold by newspapers, TV, local radio and magazines; it appears on bill-boards and at trade shows. If volume and price in any of these media are affected significantly by any of the others, they have to be considered to be part of the same market.

In the ordinary way, the better measure of market share is by reference to volume of goods sold. Where there is a wide variety of different products offered in a single market, however, the measurement of share may have to be by sales value, because of the difficulties of assessing relative volumes of different types of goods—hyacinth bulbs against garden gnomes, for instance.

## Tactical terms

At the tactical level there are a number of terms that need explanation. '*Vertical integration*' is important and indicates the extent to which the business itself undertakes the various stages in the production of the finished product. Figure 3.1 in Chapter 3 illustrates a number of such stages and the more of these that the business undertakes, the more vertically integrated it is said to be.[5] Such integration may be described as '*downstream*', i.e. starting from the manufacturing process and moving down through distribution to the ultimate customer, or '*upstream*' towards primary extraction or harvesting.

A measure of vertical integration is '*value added*'. Value added is, as the name suggests, the value added to a product by a process that alters its form, location or availability, such as manufacture of components, assembly, distribution and so on.[6] It is measured by deducting the cost of bought-in supplies and services from the sales value. Broadly, the more processes that a business undertakes in relation to a particular product, the higher the potential value added will be. Thus, for a business that did everything for itself (an impossibility), value added would be equal to sales value.

'*Productivity*' is a concept which has had whole books written around it and whole institutes formed to study it.[7] It is basically concerned with how much of a product—either in volume or value—a person or a machine, or a combination of the two, can produce. The purpose of measuring productivity is to seek for greater efficiency, by increasing unit output and/or reducing unit cost. For any business, therefore, the definition will be affected by the context:

- in a corrugated case materials mill, the area of liner produced per machine;
- in a corrugated case making factory, the number of cases made from the raw material (liner) used;
- in an advertising department, column inches of space sold per salesperson of per £ of sales costs.[8]

Increasing the productivity of a business in the UK in many instances necessarily implies redundancy. Politicians who demand full employment and competitive costing in the same breath as they demand higher wages for the work force, are totally inconsistent. '*Redundancy*' is well understood, being the condition where a job is no longer a necessary part of the value added process. '*Severance*' is a term sometimes used interchangeably with this. Other terms used in the productivity context are '*labour intensity*' and '*investment (or capital) intensity*'. These last two terms are sometimes thought of as mutually exclusive, i.e. a business has to be one or the other. This is not so, because both are measures of utilization, labour in the one case and capital in the other, and it is quite possible to be both labour and capital intensive. Some printing plants where chronic overmanning has existed and excessive machine capacity has been installed over the past decades are a particular example. Specifically, capital or investment intensity is normally measured as the historic cost of fixed assets compared to sales, though some prefer to try to get closer to the ongoing cost by taking depreciation to value added. Labour intensity may be assessed as employment costs to sales or value added, actual number of heads being largely irrelevant so long as total costs are encompassed. Such measures as these are normally used to make comparisons with competitors, to see whether the business is performing better or worse than others in the market place.

## Performance measures

The targets that are attached to tactics under the foregoing framework will tend to be specific measures of performance. While most are self-explanatory, this is an area where a wide variety of choice over terminology may occur. As will be discussed in Chapter 16, the returns that the business yields on the assets and money invested are important ratios of performance. Some analysts will refer to 'return on investment' (ROI), while others prefer 'return on capital employed' (ROCE) or even 'return on gross capital employed' (ROGCE). The term most commonly used in this book will be '*return on trading capital*' (ROTC), being profit before interest and tax ('*trading profit*') as a percentage of trading capital. '*Trading capital*' is the sum of fixed assets at historic depreciated cost, plus working capital. '*Working capital*' is limited, in this context, to trade receivables and payables (debtors and creditors) and inventories (stocks and work in progress).

'*Return on sales*' (ROS) is another ratio commonly adopted, being the trading profit as a percentage of sales. The word '*margin*' is often used interchangeably with ROS and this may be '*gross margin*' where the calculation is made at the gross profit level. 'Value added to sales' is also an important ratio, but its meaning is clear from the definition of value added given above.

In the production area '*capacity utilization*' is a useful measure. The '*capacity*' of a plant is the maximum output that it can sustain with facilities normally in operation, current technology, work rules, manning levels, shifts worked, etc. Capacity may, therefore, be limited by labour considerations as well as by machine outputs. Its utilization is the actual output expressed as a percentage of the maximum output.

## Growth

Another measure of progress in business is growth. How fast is the business developing? When analysts speak of 'growth', there is often a considerable ambiguity about what they mean. Is it sales growth, profit growth, growth in earnings, assets, equity, or what? All these may be important. If business constituted a set of fixed relationships, it would not matter which one was chosen as it could be used as a substitute for all. Since the factors influencing commercial activity are constantly changing relative to one another, however, and since it is often quite small differences that are critical, the planner must be aware of these differences. In the context of growth, this requires the use of a variety of the measurements referred to.

These growth criteria are expressed as year upon year changes, reductions being treated as negative growth. Four of the principal measures are:

- *Sales growth*    This may reflect change in either volume or value of sales; changes in volume are often referred to as '*real*' growth as they exclude any element of inflation.
- *Profit growth*    This may be examined at a number of levels, e.g. gross profit, trading profit. It is only rarely assessed in '*real*' terms (that is, discounted for inflation).
- *Earnings growth*    '*Earnings*' are taken as profits attributable to shareholders, i.e. after interest and tax. For unincorporated businesses, for 'shareholders' read 'proprietors'. Some analysts exclude extraordinary items in measuring this growth, as these will distort the annual trends. This is a matter of choice according to the frequency of extraordinaries (in some businesses they occur with alarming regularity) and to the question that the commentator is considering. If past performance is being examined, they should probably be taken into account, if future potential is being considered, they might be ignored while calculating the trend and then added back. Earnings growth is one of the most important factors in the market's assessment of the value of a company or business (see Chapter 10).
- *Equity growth*    '*Equity*' is that part of the total value of the company owned by shareholders. In this context, the value of the company may include 'intangibles', e.g. patents, know-how and goodwill, though when calculating other ratios such as gearing, these may be excluded (see below).

## Environmental factors

In considering the impact of the external world upon business, the terms of economics are employed. For a detailed review of these, see generally, the Penguin *Dictionary of Economics*.[9] Many of the terms are defined and discussed in detail in Chapter 8. At this stage, the only comments are these:

- A distinction is made between '*macro-*' and '*micro*'economics. The first refers to large-scale systems, i.e. at the national or global level; the second is concerned with individual markets or market sectors. There is, however, no clear frontier between the two.
- '*Trade cycles*' are a characteristic of both macro- and micro-systems. As the words imply, the level of economic activity cycles up and down over a relatively well-defined period of time—four to five years is the norm. These cyclical movements have to be distinguished from '*trends*' which define the overall direction in which the economy is moving over the period under review, irrespective of short-term fluctuations.

- There are a number of terms used in connection with cycles which are shown in Fig. 2.1. These are self-explanatory.
- Much has been said in recent years about 'supply-side' economics. From the point of view of the buyer in a market place, the goods or services sold to the buyer represent the *'supply-side'* of that person's business. From the seller's perspective however, the buyer is on the *'demand-side'* of the seller's business. The same transaction may, therefore, be viewed from either angle and the term only defines that aspect of the market on which policies are focused.

## Financial matters

In financial planning, the terms used will be familiar to accountants. Of particular importance are the constraints imposed upon business plans by the debt–equity ratio or by the need to avoid dilution of shareholders' interests.

*'Debt–equity ratio'* represents the relationship between financing of a company by lenders and shareholders. *'Debt'* is defined as including short-term loans and overdrafts, and is also reduced by cash or short-term investments which may be turned into cash when necessary. Equity is normally calculated by excluding goodwill (or 'cost of control'). There is argument about whether items such as deferred tax or minorities should be included in equity. The importance of such exclusions is entirely dependent upon what planners are trying to measure, and also on whether they have access to enough information to enable them to be consistent in their definition. If, therefore, their sole object is

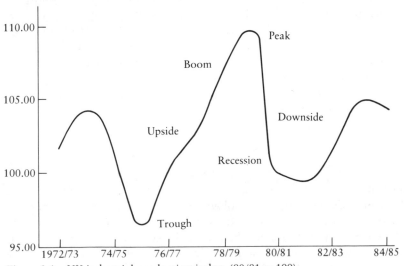

**Figure 2.1**   UK industrial production index. (80/81 = 100)

to measure their own business' vulnerability, they may adopt as detailed an analysis as they wish. If the purpose is to look at competitors, planners will be constrained by what the Extel cards or the Datastream, or other data base they are using, will tell them.

The terms 'gearing' or 'leverage' are also used in this context. If the debt–equity ratio is 50 per cent, this means that the business is one-third geared or leveraged, i.e. one-third of the total value is represented by loans and two-thirds by equity.

In this context, another useful measure of vulnerability of a business is *interest cover*, i.e. the number of times that profit before interest and tax covers the total interest payable. At present, six times would be considered prudent. This measure is useful for businesses such as publishing whose balance sheets show a lot of goodwill (which is not included in the traditional equity calculation). Borrowing up to the value of the tangible assets and even beyond may be perfectly safe because of the high returns on those assets. In such cases, interest cover is the only appropriate measure.

'*Dilution*' describes the reduction in value of the existing shareholders' interests when more shares are issued to other persons as, for example, when a business is bought for shares. If the earnings per share (EPS) of the new business (calculated by dividing its earnings by the number of shares issued for its acquisition) are less than the EPS of the acquirer, this will reduce the combined EPS. Suppose Business X has a million shares in issue and the EPS is £2.50. If 100 000 new shares are issued to acquire a business with earnings of £190 000, the EPS of the newly acquired business is only £1.90. The two businesses together produce earnings of £2 690 000, which gives a combined EPS of £2.445. The old shareholders suffer a drop in EPS of over 5p. Their interest in the earnings of the business has been diluted by the new shares issued. In the same way, it is possible to dilute the shareholders' interest in the capital value of the company.

Finally, a word about the meaning of '*monetary*': this refers to anything—assets, liabilities or capital—whose value is fixed in units of currency, regardless of the change in value of that currency.[10] This has particular relevance in the control of '*monetary working capital*' (that part of working capital designated in money terms). In this book the term generally is used to refer to trade debtors and trade creditors alone.[11]


## Conclusion

The above brief discussion of terminology sets the scene for the description of the structure of business and its objectives and the strategic and tactical options which flow from this. Other items than those defined are used in the normally accepted way and reference should be made to standard dictionaries and glossaries. One final caveat. When discussing such matters with others, it is important to be clear that each one means the same thing. But having clarified this, it is unnecessary to fuss about the words actually being used!

## Notes

1. T. O'Dell, *Daily Economic Telex*, Phillips & Drew, London, 26 September 1985.
2. D. French, *Dictionary of Accounting Terms*, Institute of Chartered Accountants in England & Wales, London, 1985. G. Bannock, R. E. Baxter and R. Rees, *Dictionary of Economics*, Penguin, Harmondsworth, 1972.
3. Ciba-Geigy use 'leitbild', see C. Lorenz, 'Explosive chemistry sparks a management revolution', The *Financial Times*, London, 5 December 1979, reprinted in book form under the title *Strategic Management and Planning in an Uncertain World*. For examples of the use of 'mission' or 'overarching goal', see D. L. Bradford and A. R. Cohen, *Managing for Excellence*, Wiley, New York, 1984.
4. S. Schoeffler, Founder and first Managing Director of Strategic Planning Institute, Boston, Mass. originated this definition. See also Chapter 5 and references.
5. R. Rumelt, *Strategy, Structure and Economic Performance*, Harvard University Press, Cambridge, Mass., 1974, pp. 19–23.
6. B. Cox, 'Value added and the management accountant', *Handbook of Management Accounting*, Gower Press, Aldershot, Hants, 1983.
7. For example, the American Productivity Center in Houston, Texas (one of five US productivity organizations) or the National Productivity Institute in S. Africa.
8. For a more detailed, but reasonably succinct description, see B. T. Gale, 'Productivity benchmarks', *The Pimsletter on Business Strategy* no. 21, The Strategic Planning Institute, Boston, Mass.
9. *Dictionary of Economics*, op. cit.
10. *Current Cost Accounting*, ED 18, Accounting Standards Committee, The Institute of Chartered Accountants in England & Wales, London, 1976, p. 25.
11. For a detailed definition, however, see *Current Cost Accounting*, SSAP 16, 'Accounting Standards 1984/85', The Institute of Chartered Accountants in England & Wales, London, 1985, p. 312.

# 3

# Business structure

### Vertical integration

Business is a series of interconnected markets. It is common to think of the whole process as starting, for instance, in mines or forests and finishing in car sales rooms or on the newsagents' stands. The traditional linkages are drawn as in Fig. 3.1. This sort of diagram is useful in showing how businesses are vertically integrated, their products moving through the various stages from primary production to the ultimate consumer; but this is not the whole story. The mines and forestry businesses take supplies, too—power, transport, capital equipment—and the customers who buy from the garage or the newsagent are also normally part of some other chain of production. Indeed, the lumberjack, working in the forest, will have his own copy of a newspaper which he could have been instrumental in producing. Furthermore, at each point in the chain, other markets are involved, such as capital equipment and labour.

It is evident, therefore, that no business is isolated from the rest of the community and that there is no industrial 'big bang' from which all production originates, nor, at the other end of the chain, some commercial Olympus where the gods enjoy consumerism unconstrained without lifting a finger in the service of toiling humanity! The commercial world is not a chain, but a network.

### The business cluster

The structure of any particular cluster of businesses in the network fits within the total system like a molecule in a chemical compound. Figure 3.2 shows such a cluster, with a particular business at the centre of its immediate markets. Business (B) is the market place for those supplying raw materials (R), labour (L), capital goods (G) and finance (F) and, in turn, it supplies its own customers (C). The arrows show the direction in which goods and services flow.

This expresses the most important connections. Thus, Jack Robinson's factory (called Plinmo, short for plastic injection moulding) is in the market for supplies of PVC, its raw material, plus energy and many other items. It competes with the local motor repair garage and brewery depot for labour and has to go to the main extrusion machinery manufacturers for its equipment (capital goods). If it is an independent business, it will be in the market for capital and

18

**Figure 3.1** The value chain

loans and its financiers will be its bankers as well as its backers. Its own customers are local authorities, builders, builders' merchants and others in the construction industry who use plastic pipes. Many of the customers could be overseas—there is a significant, though volatile, export market for products of this nature.

There are some further complications: it is possible that a business may be in competition with its own suppliers. For example, a TV company that advertises newspapers is also competing with them to sell advertising space; or a paper-maker that is also a pulp producer, may sell to rival paper mills the pulp that it manufactures. This does not, however, affect the basic structure described, though it may very well influence competitive tactics. A case in point are the Scandinavian suppliers of pulp and paper to the UK market who have been able from time to time to squeeze UK paper-makers by the manipulation of the prices of these two products in the market place. The diagram in Fig. 3.2,

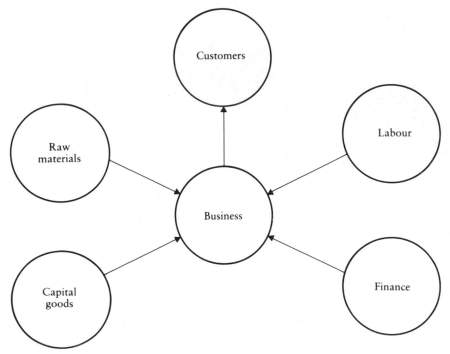

**Figure 3.2**    The business cluster

therefore, simplifies what is a very complex network of suppliers and customers.

## Translating the business structure into profit and loss

The market places shown above—and indeed, all the connected markets—represent the specific influences that affect the way in which a business operates. Accounting conventions translate these influences into both the profit and loss account and the balance sheet. Figure 3.3 links the market places and the profit and loss structures, using a few of the major items to demonstrate the connections. This is a very simplified example and does not attempt to capture the complexity of the real situation.

### THE BUSINESS STRUCTURE AND SALES

The sales shown in Fig. 3.3 are a direct result of the activity of the business in the customer market place. The revenue varies according to price, volume and mix. The prices charged will ultimately reflect what the market will bear and in theory, by lowering prices, a higher volume may be achieved. This does not

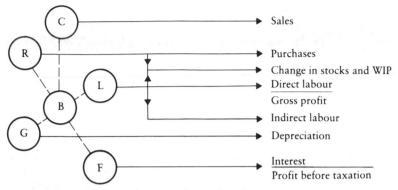

**Figure 3.3**   Business structure and the profit and loss account

always happen in practice and the question of market tactics will be explored in Chapter 7.

The third element, mix, is often difficult to pin-point in sales forecasts. Generally, the solution is to throw this factor in with price and not to try to analyse further. While the monetary expression of sales conceals very complex operations of the business in the customer market place, in planning it is enough to adopt a fairly simple approach.

BUSINESS STRUCTURE AND COSTS

The next line on the basic profit and loss account deals with direct costs, that is, relating to markets in which the business is itself the customer. These costs encompass a wide variety of purchases of goods and services. They will largely comprise raw materials and energy costs. Some businesses may, however, buy in a substantial amount of services, e.g. a publisher will contract out its printing. For these purposes, this can be treated as fundamentally of the same nature as purchase of raw materials.

Looking at the specific items included in this category, the market for energy in the UK is to a degree oligopolistic. Certainly during periods of shortage, there was little opportunity to wheel and deal except on very large contracts for oil supplies. The position has changed recently to bring oil into line with other raw materials. Many products such as paper and steel are tradables. They are open to strong international competition and, if the UK is to support an industry of its own, it has to compete with the best overseas practice. Plastics are also in this category. With the exception of some very specialized grades, there is a variety of foreign as well as domestic suppliers. The level of effectiveness of buying in the market place will be felt immediately in higher or lower costs and will either go straight through to the bottom line of the profit and loss account, or enable/force the business to raise/reduce prices, thereby influencing volumes of goods sold and, ultimately, profit.

Changes in the value of raw materials also find their way into the inventory account and are charged to profit and loss. The way in which market change is shown varies according to the method of accounting adopted. LIFO (last in, first out) where inventories are charged on the basis of the latest cost means that the business takes the full shock of inflation as it occurs. The alternative method of FIFO (first in, first out) results in a profit and loss account that does not carry the up-to-date cost of raw materials, while the balance sheet includes these items at an over-value.

Continuing down the simplified profit and loss account, the next major influence is the labour market. The impact there is somewhat different from that in the raw materials sector in that market forces tend to be more difficult to unravel. A plant that is strongly unionized on the traditional pattern will probably pay over the average rate per unit of output—not necessarily because wage rates are that much higher, but because of overmanning, restrictive practices and similar factors which contribute to lower productivity. Equally, low investment levels may also affect cost per unit output, where inefficient, old equipment may be incapable of producing the same output per man hour as more up-to-date machinery. Labour costs affect the profit and loss account both at the direct and the indirect level and are also an important part of the work-in-progress element of inventories.

The capital goods sector will have a more long-term effect on the profit and loss account. Fixed assets, purchased less often, are charged to the profit and loss account through depreciation, generally on a historic cost basis. Inflation and the state of the capital goods market may, therefore, have a substantial hidden effect upon the business. The problems of coping with inflation in this context are considered in Chapter 8.

Finally, when looking at the bare bones of the profit and loss account, is the item for interest. This is a factor which, over the last 10 years has been moving around, not just as a function of commercial activity, but also as a result of governmental and speculative pressures, both strongly influenced by and influencing exchange rates. It is, therefore, a very tangled part of the net and a part that requires considerable expertise to begin to see the directions in which some of the strands lead. At this point, all that is needed is to recognize the significant effect on earnings and cash flow that the financial markets may have.

### Plinmo's profit and loss account

Plinmo's profit and loss account might, therefore, be built up as shown in Table 3.1—this is based on the actual experience of a small company, though the financing computations are only broad estimates. The figures are given over a five-year period to give a feel for the trends.

The bar chart in Fig. 3.4 has been prepared to indicate the way in which some of the individual items have changed, relative to one another. This

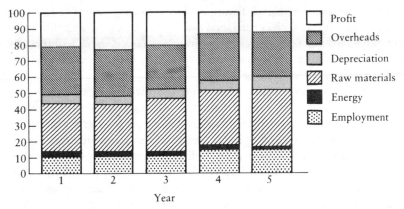

**Figure 3.4**  Cost and profit percentages of sales

**Table 3.1**  Framework profit and loss account, Plinmo Limited

| £'000s | Year 1 | 2 | 3 | 4 | 5 |
|---|---|---|---|---|---|
| Total sales | 1925 | 2231 | 2490 | 2493 | 2604 |
| Direct costs: | | | | | |
| employment | 218 | 258 | 283 | 366 | 391 |
| energy | 51 | 61 | 67 | 68 | 66 |
| raw materials | 576 | 652 | 831 | 852 | 903 |
| Gross profit | 1080 | 1260 | 1309 | 1207 | 1244 |
| Indirect costs: | | | | | |
| depreciation | 98 | 111 | 128 | 145 | 201 |
| other overheads | 570 | 641 | 684 | 730 | 728 |
| Trading profit | 412 | 508 | 497 | 332 | 315 |
| Financial items: | | | | | |
| interest | 40 | 43 | 18 | 20 | 54 |
| taxation | 125 | 227 | 201 | 24 | 45 |
| dividend | 100 | 100 | 100 | 100 | 100 |
| Retained earnings | 147 | 138 | 178 | 188 | 116 |

emphasizes that changes in the market places are by no means uniform and will vary against one another over time.

## Business structure and the balance sheet
The balance sheet is also affected by the market places, but because of the nature of its make-up, the influences here are more long-term; at least, that was

the view before the onset of high inflation in the early 'seventies. The fact that the balance sheet may only be constructed once or twice a year and that fixed assets are purchased less frequently than current assets conceals the impact of market forces on the structure of the business. As stated, the effect of inflation will be reviewed in depth in Chapter 8.

In the mean time, the important connections are traced in Fig. 3.5. The first two items shown in the figure, cash and receivables, like sales, are the result of activity in the customer market place. The level of receivables as a proportion of sales will tend to vary according to the health of the economy generally; in periods of recession, debts become more difficult to collect. Equally this may affect the provision for bad debts, though this is not shown on the diagram. Further, the time for settling may be extended to help customers through cash crises. Payables, which are a function of raw materials and other supply markets, including capital goods, are the other side of the coin and in a crisis, the business may unilaterally decide to take extra time to settle. The balance to be kept between receivables and payables is an important feature of finance planning and is addressed in Chapter 10.

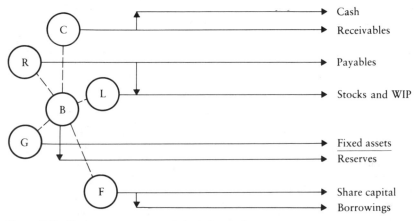

**Figure 3.5**   Business structure and the balance sheet

The impact of bought-in supplies and labour costs on inventories has been discussed above.

The value of fixed assets in the balance sheet is initially the price paid for the plant, land and buildings, etc. in the capital goods (or property) market. There is always a mixture of old and new in the balance sheet. This item, therefore, only imperfectly reflects what is going on at the present, unless depreciation is charged on a replacement basis and there is an adequate replacement provision to give an idea of what it would cost to replant to required strategic standards; replacement depreciation on its own is not enough as it only gives a one-year

**Table 3.2**  Framework balance sheet, Plinmo Limited

| £'000s | | Year 1 | | 2 | | 3 | | 4 | | 5 |
|---|---|---|---|---|---|---|---|---|---|---|
| Fixed assets | | 745 | | 753 | | 823 | | 1088 | | 1260 |
| Working capital: | | | | | | | | | | |
| stocks and WIP | 370 | | 424 | | 469 | | 489 | | 498 | |
| debtors | 385 | | 436 | | 511 | | 507 | | 598 | |
| creditors | (290) | | (346) | | (359) | | (350) | | (405) | |
| | | 465 | | 514 | | 621 | | 646 | | 691 |
| Trading capital | | 1210 | | 1267 | | 1444 | | 1734 | | 1951 |
| Other payables (tax, etc.) | | (125) | | (230) | | (204) | | (28) | | (49) |
| Cash | | 9 | | 55 | | 30 | | 5 | | 3 |
| Total assets | | 1094 | | 1092 | | 1270 | | 1711 | | 1905 |
| Borrowings: | | | | | | | | | | |
| 9% loan stock | | 250 | | 250 | | 250 | | 250 | | 250 |
| overdraft and | | | | | | | | | | |
| short-term loans | | 145 | | 5 | | 5 | | 258 | | 336 |
| Shareholders interests: | | | | | | | | | | |
| share capital | | 300 | | 300 | | 300 | | 300 | | 300 |
| profit and loss a/c | | 399 | | 537 | | 715 | | 903 | | 1019 |
| | | 1094 | | 1092 | | 1270 | | 1711 | | 1905 |

snapshot of the situation. Sometimes there is a big backlog as a result of restrictions on spending in previous years.

Reserves represent past profits and losses of the business, whether from revenue or capital transactions, and are not a direct result of any specific market place. The final items in Fig. 3.5, share capital and loans, are influenced by the financial markets and the questions this raises are discussed in Chapter 10.

Table 3.2 shows a framework balance sheet which has been built up for Plinmo Limited. The asset side of the balance sheet, like the trading account, is based on actual experience and is presented in a format that highlights trading capital before showing the items relating to financing. The liabilities side is constructed to be able to use it for considering the position of Plinmo as a total company, but it is not based on fact.

Thus, the profit and loss account and balance sheet summarize, in very broad terms, what has happened, or is projected to happen in the various market places in which the business operates. Each set of figures is a snapshot in time, but by displaying a series of annual results, a feel for the dynamics of the business may be obtained. For a full understanding, however, all the main external markets as well as the internal production and personnel characteristics have to be explored. This takes time and experience. Armed, nevertheless, with an appreciation of the general structure of business and knowing a lot about the relevant markets, the management is ready to embark upon the formal process of planning.

# 4

# Objectives

### The need for objectives
The following paragraph appeared in the annual report and accounts of a UK corporation in 1969. It was a statement of objectives and expressed the desire:

> To be a prosperous and expanding international corporation, maintaining leadership in our field of business and meeting the reasonable requirements of the public, our shareholders and our employees, within the constraints set by the social obligations of our times.[1]

In the late 'sixties, there was a cult for such expressions of mission by large corporations. For most business people, this was a very new approach to management. Up to the middle of the decade, few had paused to enquire what they were in business for; it was enough to be profitable with a cash flow that ensured survival. In those heady days of growth, the majority of corporations were comfortably within those guidelines, however wild the management. There had been a handful of spectacular crashes, like the John Bloom washing machine empire. But the pressure of an adverse environment had not yet begun to exert any real discipline.

By the late 'sixties, however, the UK had been through a number of squeezes and freezes. Social unrest and a growing assertiveness by individuals during a period which saw a levelling off in growth and downturn in productivity, led to a reappraisal among uneasy corporate leaders as to what the business was all about. Worries about the damage that uncommitted employees and a very hostile environment could do, led boards of directors to publish statements of objectives in their annual reports. By asserting explicitly that they were concerned about people, they hoped to avert the evil eye of social change.

Remarkably, some still do include such statements, but the practice has largely died out because it was never made into a *practical* tool for management. How could a statement such as that above be used? It means nothing except perhaps as a public relations puff. In no way does it help to set the direction of management. The only purpose of setting objectives is to provide a proper framework for running the business. Without objectives, plans cannot be laid systematically. Plans have to be aimed at getting the business somewhere, and objectives say where this is.

This assertion is strongly supported by the analogous case of a military campaign. If the commander-in-chief fails to include in his orders that he intends to make a broad sweep through the Low Countries and northern France in order to roll up the French flank from the left and spearhead towards Paris, all his subordinate commanders will have to guess at what his objectives are and chaos will follow. Such a failure prevailed with the Russian divisions in Prussia in August 1914[2] when a number of the units fought with considerable bravery. Since the command was not competent enough to specify and communicate clear and credible objectives, local commanders were on their own. Defeat was inevitable, despite significantly superior numbers, because the other side knew better what it was doing.

## Clarity and adequacy

Objectives, therefore, are necessary and they must be clear. Clarity will most readily be achieved if the objectives are kept short. The statement quoted above was only a small part of the whole. Other corporations have taken several pages to express their respective missions in their annual report to share-holders. As a mechanism for guiding the overall direction this cannot be used.

On the other hand, some stated corporate objectives are admirably brief, but in the planning context are still not helpful. IBM strives for 'customer service', while General Electric (the US one) claims that 'progress is our most important product'.[3] These mottoes may be effective in enthusing the work force and set-ting the style of the corporation,[4] but they do not help the staff in planning the future direction of the business, nor do they provide the chief executive with any reasonable yardstick to measure how closely the business is getting to achieving its objectives. If either of these corporations relied solely on such statements, they would have problems. Clearly they do not as both are highly successful: they have indeed very extensive planning processes with carefully thought-through objectives.

If mottoes are nevertheless to be in fashion, it would not be a bad thing to return to the old-fashioned notion that the purpose of business is to create wealth, and then to try to develop some specific objectives that will help to-wards this—for example, return on investment, earnings growth, cash flow levels and the like.

## Alternative corporate objectives

The creation of wealth is not universally accepted as the criterion for commer-cial activity, though in this book it is taken to be so. There are other options which may be adopted, e.g.:

● to maximize employment—some state corporations would appear to aim for this;

- to provide a social service—state railways and transport are specific examples; they are subsidized in all countries, even the United States;
- to be the biggest—shareholders of some corporations that grew massively in sales and assets during the 'sixties and early 'seventies could be forgiven, as earnings per share dropped like a stone, for wondering whether aggrandizement of the Board was not really the purpose of the game.

Where such alternative objectives are adopted, the need to create wealth will act as a constraint. If, in pursuit of such other aims (say for instance, full employment), the company fails to make enough profit, it may collapse economically. The unrestricted pursuit of full employment is not possible—a lesson that has been very harshly learned in the British economy.

### Describing the business sector

Return on investment and similar sorts of criteria are not as stimulating as mottoes, but they do begin to describe more clearly what the business is trying to do in quantified terms. However, they still do not adequately describe the territory over which the troops will be fighting. There is a need for a general description of the market sectors and the countries in which the organization intends to do business. How closely such factors are defined will depend on the state of the business at the time. In practice it will also depend on how closely the chief executive is prepared to bind himself in advance, but the issue of dealing with bosses who prefer to conceal their hand is considered later (in Chapter 17).

There is, nevertheless, no point in being so precise that it cramps the development of the firm. So it is probably better for Jack Robinson, with his plastics factory, to say that he is in the plastic conversion business, rather than in the manufacture of plastic pipes. His move into large mouldings would make nonsense of objectives expressed in the latter terms. Equally, the likelihood that he would move into the manufacture and supply of raw material plastics is so remote that he need not draw his boundaries as broadly as 'plastics' alone.

Sir James Forbes's conglomerate presents a different problem in this context. No multi-business organization should limit itself in its statement of objectives to specific market sectors, unless it is completely certain that it will not want to move outside such areas in the foreseeable future. It may—and should—specify in the strategies it adopts to fulfil its objectives, the markets it will be in, but in principle, the whole world may be open to it. The corporation might, however, be more certain of its geographical borders and indicate that its principal business 'shall be conducted in North America and northern Europe', or 'our sphere of operation shall be the Pacific basin'. There seems to be a somewhat longer time-scale when adding to location than when expanding products and services.

## The time horizon of objectives

This question of time-scale is important, because objectives should be as near timeless as practicable. There are goals and targets that have to be discarded (as goals/targets) once they are achieved. In World War I, had the Schlieffen Plan proposed only to break through the Belgian fortresses at Liège, this would not have sufficed as a guideline for very long. This was accomplished in a very short space of time after the invasion of Belgium, and after that the troops needed further directions on where to go. So, in the commercial context, winning a major contract, overtaking a competitor, hitting a particular return on investment may all be too short-term.

The statement: 'The achievement of return and growth equivalent to UK multinational corporations in the upper quartile of performance' is of this sort. If the company is well managed, it will soon get there. What should its objectives be then? It sets new ones—perhaps substituting the upper decile for upper quartile, but it might even attain this excellence fairly quickly. This type of approach is useful, provided that it acts as a rallying point for management to get that little bit of extra profit, cash flow or return on investment out of the business. However, an objective should be something that does not change too often, not least because it can take a long time to sink into the corporate consciousness, and the signposts ought to be left unchanged for as long as possible.

## Relevance

Objectives still have to be immediately relevant to the operation, notwithstanding their timelessness. Comparison with other businessess on a large or even on a small scale may be futile. Jack Robinson is not concerned with being in the top quartile, he is far too small, but he could aim to match the performance of similar businesses. Going further down the scale to market stallholders, east-end whelk sellers are totally unconcerned with what anyone else in the business is doing so long as they are not competing on their patch. It would be ridiculous to suggest to them that they should aim to do anything other than sell as many whelks as possible, diversifying only into cockles and mussels in season. Maybe they want to become another Wheelers, but at their scale of development, an over-grandiose objective is useless. The objective has to be relevant to the type and scale of business.

In summary, therefore, objectives should be:

- *Measurable*   They provide a yardstick for all actions.
- *Clear*   Avoid obscuring the direction and issues, particularly by saying too much.
- *Limiting*   They must set some real-world boundaries for the business.
- *Long-term*   They should not be achievable too quickly.
- *Relevant*   They must fit the business.

## The importance of management style

Another important factor influencing objectives is management style—how the business is going to be run. This again is not a reference to the generalized sort of statement that opened this chapter because that did not let anyone into the secret of how it was intended the company would be managed, except perhaps where it used the word 'reasonable' to qualify the way in which management was going to act. (That, in any event, implied 'reasonable' so far as the corporation was concerned, but not necessarily in the eyes of the public, the shareholders or employees, so maybe the company was not such a soft touch after all!)

This question of style is all to do with the culture of the corporation. It is normally strongly influenced by the chief executive and the team of people round him or her, as well as by its traditions, nationality, etc. Thus, in dealing with suppliers, customers, staff and the community generally, the management may adopt very different attitudes compared to the corporation across the street. These attitudes necessarily act as a constraint upon the attainment of the objectives, particularly in so far as they are expressed in profit terms.

Sir James Forbes might say:

> We can't close this plant down at the moment. There's far too much unemployment in the area.

> Pornography may be the most profitable sector of publishing there is, but count us out.

> This corporation will not get involved in a contested acquisition bid.

> We will not go for that tax dodge: we will avoid, but not evade taxation.

All these are statements that have actually been made at various times by directors of important public companies. They all limit the corporate endeavour to optimize towards its objectives. But business people, whether hired hands or owners, have to observe the constraints imposed by the various communities within which they live—the town from which the labour force is drawn, the family, social or church group which affects their moral standards, the commercial and financial circles within which they pass their business days.

Another feature of management style is the extent to which the business is to be managed in a centralized, decentralized, or even remote way. There are many factors that dictate how closely the chief executive and the team can be involved in direct management on the shop floor. A large organization such as Sir James Forbes's conglomerate must delegate a large part of the task. But both he and Jack Robinson can choose the extent to which the businesses they run are wholly owned or shared. Jack Robinson can go in for joint ventures, sub-contracts and agencies, rather than doing everything in his own factory and through his own sales force. Sir James may take majority or minority positions in certain businesses as well as holding others as 100 per cent subsidiaries. The reasons are often personal preferences of the management team. Unlike the more generalized features of management style referred to in the previous paragraphs, it may be useful to specify in the set of objectives the type of structure and level of ownership of any business or venture that the company is prepared to contemplate. It is not necessary to do so, but it may add some clarification of what the business is trying to achieve.

## Constraints

In addition to management style, there are a variety of other constraints that are imposed on business, rather than adopted as a conscious choice. Many of these are enforced through legislation, e.g. monopolies and fair trading; some by delegated powers, as are the planning controls exercised by local authorities; others by regulations, such as the Stock Exchange rules for quoted companies; or by pressure groups like the institutional committees; or directly within the company by trade unions.

Looking again at the business structure described in Chapter 3, we have to add some circles to represent additional influences of this nature. On the right-hand side of Fig. 4.1 are shown some of the ways in which the factors concerned affect business. 'Go' stands for 'government' and 'Co' for 'community'.

These examples suggest only a very few of the constraints that affect business, but they illustrate the different types. Thus, most product and service markets are the subject of monopoly or anti-trust legislation. An objective to be the only supplier of motor cars or motor insurance in the UK is not achievable. Even if it were possible by effective trading to get there, few governments would tolerate such a position for a private company for long. In Britain,

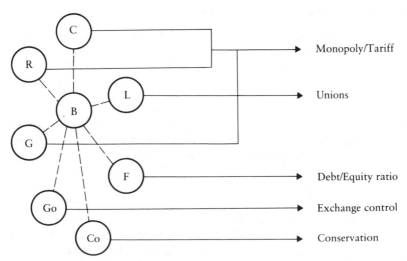

**Figure 4.1** Constraints on the business

nationalized corporations have a high level of monopoly, but none is complete and privatization is present government policy. In France, the nationalized banks were still kept as separate entities which were required to compete.

Another obvious area of government intervention is in keeping foreign goods out of the country by tariff (and indeed by non-tariff) barriers. An objective to penetrate a national market whose government was determined to exclude newcomers would be unlikely to prove fruitful. Equally, a project to develop a product that was highly pollutant (mercury- or chrome-based processes are specific cases) or obnoxious (in some communities, sex shops are unaccept-able), would run up against community lobbies. Furthermore, expansion into territories where it is virtually impossible to get any cash out again, either because of specific exchange control regulations or just because of the way in which business is done in that location, cannot be the best way to seek to de-velop business.

Finally, in the examples given above, there is the question of cash resources. How much cash has the business to implement its strategies? This may be measured by looking at the debt–equity ratio. If the business needs more money than it is generating through trading, it may be possible to fund it by borrowing more, though such a situation may indicate a fundamental weakness. The policy options as to the level of this ratio are considered in Chapter 10; it is suf-ficient here to comment that institutional investors and lenders are concerned to ensure that the company in which they have invested is not too heavily bor-rowed. The same principles apply when bank managers are deciding on how much they are prepared to advance to small businesses. The availability of funds from such sources is a major constraint upon the scale of operations and hence upon the objectives of the business.

To summarize, constraints may be classified as:

- *Financial*   Has the company enough resources to do what it wants?
- *Stylistic*   Are any business policies or practices a bar to actions?
- *Legal*   Are there specific or general barriers?
- *Political*   Are there external inhibitions (including, for example, pressures exerted by trade unions)?

These limitations on what a corporation or firm may do are not just relevant at the level of setting objectives. They affect every level of decision making. Strat-egies and tactics also have to be subjected to similar tests.


### A checklist for preparing objectives

A checklist based on the foregoing discussion is useful in making a start on deciding the explicit objectives of an organization. The following is an example:

- What sort of businesses is the company in now?
- Will it concentrate on a definable business sector?
- Will it apply any territorial limits?
- Will the businesses be wholly owned, jointly owned, etc?
- What performance criteria should be applied?

The first three questions will define the products/services and locations in which the organization is intended to operate; the next deals with management style in terms of the structure of the business; the final one sets the overall criteria, such as market share, earnings per share, return on investment or any other measurement by which the performance is to be judged.

It is possible to adopt a rather more structured approach to resolving what the objectives should be, rather than this simple checklist.[5] By careful analysis of questions such as those above, some of the intuition may be eliminated, but this is a circular argument. In order to analyse effectively, it has to be with a view to achieving something. That 'something' is the set of objectives. In the end, therefore, the objectives have to be set intuitively by the top person (and their team) as a start to the planning process, though they should be reviewed from time to time against an understanding of where the company is at the time of such review.

## Objectives for Plinmo and Conglom

This description of objectives concludes with sample sets for each of Jack Robinson's plastics factory, Plinmo Limited, and Sir James Forbes's conglomerate, Conglom PLC.

Applying the checklist to Plinmo, the following could be the conclusion:

| | |
|---|---|
| 1. What business now? | Extrusion of plastic pipes; plastic injection mouldings of pipe fittings, food containers and motor accessories in the UK |
| 2. What future sectors? | Any plastic conversion business with similar production processes |
| 3. What territory? | United Kingdom |
| 4. What structure? | Wholly owned businesses |
| 5. What criteria? | —Significant market share |
| | —30 per cent return on investment |
| | —5 per cent volume growth per annum |

This is undoubtedly a mixed bag of objectives which might not stand up to the scrutiny of a logician, but what is important is whether this list sets out aims that are realistic, adequate and credible and that provide positive guidelines for the running of the business.

Likewise, Conglom might answer the questions as follows:

| | |
|---|---|
| 1. What business now? | Conglomerate concentrated in building materials, motor vehicles, communications and packaging |
| 2. What future sectors? | Any profitable sector, preferably contiguous to existing |
| 3. What territory? | North America, Western Europe, Australasia |
| 4. What structure? | Any ownership pattern, provided control can be exerted |
| 5. What criteria? | Individual businesses will have their own, including specifically, high relative market share; the corporation overall aims at steady earnings growth of the order of 5 per cent in excess of inflation per annum |

This now gives a reasonably clear idea of what Conglom is about. From the above, detailed strategies and tactics, goals and targets may be deduced in an area that is at least territorially circumscribed. The corporate staff will undoubtedly be casting around for new market sectors to examine. Would plastic conversion be an interesting sector? Should Conglom be planning a bid for Plinmo?

The next chapter takes a step further in defining market strategies and examines the ways in which both Conglom and Plinmo will deal with these issues.

## Notes

1. *Annual Report and Accounts*, International Publishing Corporation, London, 1969. The document does go on to specify fields of business and to nominate earnings per share as an objective, though all is very generalized.
2. B. W. Tuchman, *August 1914*, Constable, London, 1962.
3. T. J. Peters and R. H. Waterman Jr., *In Search of Excellence*, Harper & Row, New York, 1982.
4. D. L. Bradford and A. R. Cohen, *Managing for Excellence*, Wiley, New York, 1984.
5. R. I. Ackoff, *A Concept of Corporate Planning*, Wiley, New York, 1970, pp. 23–41.

# 5

# Market strategies

### The impact of market strategies

Strategies are the means in market terms of achieving business objectives. All business starts in the market place: without customers there is no business. There are, however, two ways of looking at customers. As was demonstrated in Chapter 3, Plinmo is the customer of extrusion machine manufacturers, PVC and other plastic suppliers, electrical and other utilities and so on. Its own customers are local authorities, builders and the like. Market strategies are expressed in relation to the latter, i.e. the customer of the business, rather than to its suppliers. The impact of the supply side is considered in Chapter 8.

Businesses can increase, reduce or maintain market share. The importance of this lies in the fact that there is a strong relationship between the market share that a business enjoys and the level of return that can be made out of the assets employed in that market. Figure 5.1, taken from the PIMS data base which incorporates the experience of over 2000 businesses, shows clearly that the higher the relative market share a business has, the higher its potential return on investment (ROI).[1] ROI, the term used by PIMS, is identical with ROTC as earlier defined (see Chapter 2). Relative market share is measured as the share of the business under investigation as a proportion of the combined shares of its three largest competitors. It is *relative* share that counts. A company with 10 per cent of a highly fragmented market may dominate it, whereas if, with the same share, it is the smallest of half a dozen operators, it is likely to be in a weak position.

High relative market share is not the only factor affording potentially high levels of profitability—there are others such as low capital intensity and high product quality, which are discussed later. Furthermore, deliberate manipulation of market share may have a different short-term effect. While investment is being made to increase share, this may cause a dip in return until the investment begins to pay off. Alternatively, deliberate shedding of share will normally result in an improved cash flow and possibly higher temporary returns as investment is reduced.

It is this last point that makes sense of strategies to reduce share deliberately. Factors imposed by the outside world such as new technology, superseding products, or subsidized foreign competition may make the position in a market untenable. In such a situation, it will be better to switch assets from an

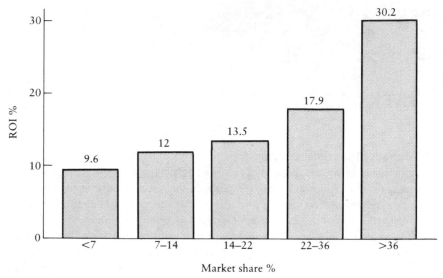

**Figure 5.1**    Market share v. profitability

unprofitable competitive sector to a different area. In other cases, where a business is making a return, but resource is needed for another area which can offer better results—and particularly where a realization will generate a better long-term cash flow than sticking with the activity—it is clearly a case for moving out of or diminishing presence in that sector.

### Strategic options

Changing market share is, therefore, the key strategic opportunity for any business. The options may be classified as shown in Fig. 5.2, though there is nothing magic in this classification. It merely offers a useful basis for the discussion. A 'Maintain' strategy means holding the existing market share. This may be a

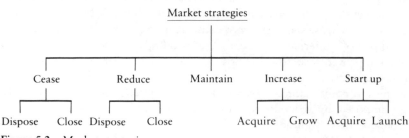

**Figure 5.2**    Market strategies

dynamic strategy if the market itself is moving fast. Conversely, it implies a shrinking investment if it is declining. In a fast growing situation, it may not be possible, in any event, to gain share.

It is often true in any rapidly expanding market that there is no adequate measure of market size to enable a strategy to be made specific in these terms. It is then impossible to do more than indicate the sort of sales volumes that are sought. In the mid-'seventies, the sale of electrically heated showers suddenly took off. It was possible to sell out the whole factory production and still leave some unsatisfied demand. There was no opportunity at that stage of development to make any accurate or even useful assessment of the total demand. Another situation where it is difficult and certainly not economically useful to make any estimate of the total sales volumes or value is in the case of exports to a multiplicity of different small markets. The amount of time devoted to investigating what may be rapidly changing situations in terms of the political, exchange and debtor climate would not be worth while.

Only when the market starts to settle down can the strategy be properly defined in share terms. But caution is needed. Once the market has settled, the cost and effort required to change market share increases substantially.[2] Those who have achieved a strong position defend it vigorously. It pays, therefore, to monitor what is going on continuously and, unless constrained by lack of resource, to keep up with and even ahead of the competition.

GROWTH STRATEGIES

The righthand side of the diagram in Fig. 5.2 indicates opportunities to expand market share, either by developing existing businesses or by starting new ones. This may be done by acquisition or by the launch of a greenfields venture. Both routes were illustrated by the activities of IPC Consumer Magazines, a UK publishing business, which acquired European Courtesy Magazines Group, a publisher of high-quality, controlled circulation consumer periodicals. The acquisition established IPC's presence in this sector of the market. This was then expanded by the launch of other glossy titles aimed at the wealthy living in the capital.

In a period of high inflation and/or considerable environmental turbulence such as the world suffered in the decade after 1973, acquisition tends to be a more favourable route, particularly in businesses with long lead times. The uncertainties of the market by the time a ten-year project comes to fruition make it worth while to pay the premium demanded for the immediate purchase of a viable existing business in the appropriate sector. There remain, none the less, good opportunities for smart operators to pick up plant cheaply as the inefficient go to the wall. There are publications that circulate details of bankrupt or liquidation stocks and plant which could be used for low-cost start-up.[3]

It remains an anomaly that some industries in their investment policies tend to adopt a lemming-like desire for self-destruction in prolonged periods of

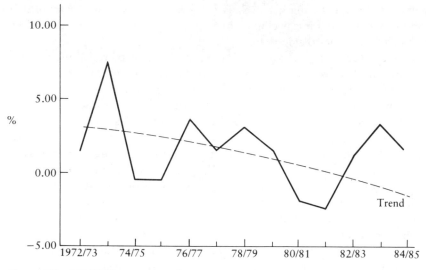

**Figure 5.3**   UK GDP percentage change per annum

recession, that is to say when economic activity shows a long-term downward trend. During these periods, conditions may improve temporarily during the upside of the trade cycle, but conversely, on the downside, there are very severe falls in demand. Figure 5.3 illustrates this concept.[4] On the upside of each trade cycle, despite the underlying direction of the trend, these industrialists perceive a new dawn of growth and plan further capacity. Plant and equipment is purchased, probably at its most expensive just as the cycle turns downwards. It then takes about four or five years to come on-stream, to coincide with the next cyclical downturn. They manage to create, in this way, a perpetual surplus capacity in the industry. Certainly the global paper-making industry seemed to follow this pattern during the traumas of the 'seventies. An improving pattern has now emerged, though there remains a surplus in certain grades.[5]

From the strategic point of view, there is no intrinsic difference between acquisition and a greenfields venture. Both are aimed at starting up or increasing presence in the market place. They have to be preceded by a view on the desirability of such expansion, before coming to conclusions about whether it is to be home-grown or bought in. So Jack Robinson, having decided he wants to get into large-scale injection moulding, has to decide whether it potentially offers a better long-term return to buy an existing business or to start up one of his own.

RETRENCHMENT STRATEGIES
On the other side of the coin are the options to reduce presence in the market.

This activity is often called 'harvesting' as it implies gathering in the investment by reduction of fixed and working capital and running the business for maximum immediate cash flow. The most dramatic way in which this may be done is by closure, i.e. stopping the activity completely and selling off the assets. These may include the customer list, which could have a value, particularly if the reason for closure has been excess capacity in the industry.

If, however, there is only a partial closure, the customer list will be the critical part to be retained and the business may reap only a poor harvest out of the equipment and buildings. Disposal of a business as a going concern may be a more fruitful alternative, if it is intended to exit from the sector completely.

## Timing

An important feature of any of the above strategies is timing. Apart from external considerations, the reason is the constraint imposed both by shortage of management and by financial resource. It is obvious that the boss and the management team will not be able to handle all the problems and opportunities simultaneously. It is not so obvious that buying and selling businesses will affect the gearing level. Generally speaking, the sale or closure of a low performance business will result in a write-off. This reduces the value of the shareholders' equity. Equally, an acquisition will probably involve the payment of a premium over the net asset value of the company acquired. If the price is in cash, this increases debt, but the goodwill acquired does not count towards equity. In these ways, both development and cut-back strategies may raise the level of debt–equity ratio excessively.

This means that priorities and a timetable have to be established, if major restructuring is proposed. It is possible to include very precise timings, such as 'mid-1986' or 'end-1988'. It is, however, most unlikely that a rigid timetable can be adhered to when outside parties are involved, as is the case with acquisitions and disposals. A somewhat vaguer programme would be sufficient, specifying actions as 'fast', 'slow' and 'medium'. With such an outline, the chief executive would at least have a general concept of the priorities attached to the various options.

## Defining the market

This discussion of strategic options has now to be anchored to reality. In view of the importance of market share, it is essential to define the market properly. The Strategic Planning Institute (SPI) of Cambridge, Mass., has done a considerable amount of work in analysing this problem. The results confirm that the important strategic unit is the 'served' market. This is 'the specific segment of the total potential market in which the business is making a serious

There are computer techniques for assisting in the resolution of such problems. Solutions were, however, being effectively reached, at least on a limited scale, by experienced managers long before computers came along. The human brain is good at juggling with problems of mix, proposing alternatives, testing the market, adjusting to the feedback and so moving towards an optimum solution. Whether it is Sir James Forbes relying on a sophisticated EDP program or Jack Robinson using his experience, the basic process remains the same:

- define the market sectors
- establish the strategies
- propose the trade-off
- test for optimization
- adjust the strategy mix

Conglom has some slight advantage in that it might be able to simulate some of the market reactions on its computer sufficiently well to avoid having to test some of the proposals in the real world, with all the attendant delays in time and the possibly traumatic consequences of getting it wrong. Similar problems arise in connection with portfolio management when deciding which out of all the businesses should be fostered, which reduced and which maintained. This and the optimization program approach are discussed in Chapters 9 and 13.

Unlike objectives, market strategies are not intuitive. They follow from the objectives as modified by the constraints referred to. They require judgement, certainly, but this is based on knowledge of the market and not on intuition. Establishing a market strategy implies a careful definition of the market place, following which, a choice may be made among the various options indicated, including timing. By their nature, strategies are not expected to be timeless, but for practical reasons, they must be capable of surviving a reasonably long time. A company that changes its strategies frequently cannot take proper long-term decisions on investment or undertake the necessarily prolonged management actions necessary to build up a presence in a market. A time-scale of the order of five years tends to be generally accepted. On the other hand, if changes in the environment or in the competitive situation force a variation in strategies, the existence of a set of strategies that is no longer applicable should not be allowed to act as a strait-jacket. Like all other parts of the planning process, they are there to give structure and direction. They do not have an existence in their own right.

## Examples of strategies

Plinmo Limited will go through such an exercise. It might propose the following set of strategies in pursuit of the objectives that were described in Chapter 4.

- Food containers          Grow share slowly to improve market position
- Plastic pipes and fittings    Maintain present share of the UK market; increase volume of exports in the medium term (no information available on market size)
- Motor accessories        Reduce share and breadth of present lines quickly; invest (probably by acquisition) in manufacture of plastic car bumpers

Conglom will have a similar strategy set for each of its four main markets with the strategies divided as above into the separate sectors of those markets in which it is doing business. It may also make proposals for moving into new business sectors; would it wish, as was queried earlier, to get into plastic conversion?

These statements of market strategies should now be translated into specific goals for the management of the separate business units. In practice, such goals will be developed in partnership with the operating managers, particularly where an integrated management system is in operation and rewards are tied to the fulfilment of objectives.

Taking Plinmo, its strategies may translate into the goals shown in Table 5.1.

**Table 5.1**  Specific goals for the management of the separate business units, Plinmo Limited

| | | | Years | | |
|---|---|---|---|---|---|
| Market sector | Strategy | Goals | 1 | 2 | 3 |
| Food containers | Grow share slowly to improve market position | Market share % | 8 | 9 | 11 |
| | | ROI % | 27 | 26 | 24 |
| | | Growth % pa. | 2 | 4 | 7 |
| Plastic pipes | Maintain present share of UK market | Market share % | 9 | 9 | 9 |
| | | ROI % | 23 | 23 | 24 |
| | | Growth % pa. | 3 | 2 | 4 |
| | Increase volume of exports over the medium term | ROI % | 31 | 30 | 33 |
| | | Growth % pa. | 5 | 9 | 10 |
| Motor accessories | Reduce share and breadth of present lines, quickly | Market share % | 7 | 5 | 3 |
| | | ROI % | 12 | 13 | 15 |
| | | Cash flow/sales % | 13 | 17 | 15 |
| | Acquire plastic car bumper manufacturer | Market share % | — | 22 | 23 |
| | | ROI % | — | 14 | 19 |
| | | Growth % pa. | — | 7 | 7 |

These goals are precise benchmarks in terms of share, return and growth (and in the case of harvesting the motor accessories business, the level of cash flow). They may be as detailed as is desired in terms of market sectors, for example they could include the respective sales volumes to be expected in each of the main export markets for plastic pipes and mouldings. They should not, however, get into the realm of tactics and targets as described in Chapter 7. At this stage, the purpose is only to set the market scene, not to go into details of costs, production, etc.

By attaching goals to the necessarily more generalized strategies, they flesh out what is expected of management without making the strategies themselves over-precise. Precision in that context would be too hampering. It is certainly possible, and expected, that goals will not be achieved in every case. Furthermore, as pointed out earlier in the specific case of acquiring or disposing of businesses, any accurate timing is very speculative. That is why, in the above example for Plinmo, a period of two years has been allowed for the fulfilment of this particular strategy. By surrounding the strategies with goals, the strategies themselves are insulated from failure and survive for a reasonable timescale. In this way, an effective framework can be prepared within which the business may be run.

## Notes

1. R. D. Buzzell *et al.*, 'Market share—a key to profitability', *Harvard Business Review*, January/February 1975.
2. R. D. Buzzell, 'Are there natural market structures?', *Journal of Marketing*, Winter 1981, pp. 42–51.
3. For example, the Business Search and Insolvency Supplement to *Venture Capital Report Journal*, Bristol.
4. The long wave cycle is discussed fully in C. Freeman (ed.), 'Technical innovation and long waves in world economic development', *Futures* vol. 13, no. 4, IPC Science and Technical Press, Guildford, 1981.
5. The forest products planning services of SRI International, Stanford, Cal., provides details world-wide of supply and demand for paper products.
6. S. Schoeffler, 'Market Position: Build, Hold or Harvest?', *Pimsletter on Business Strategy* no. 3, Strategic Planning Institute, Cambridge, Mass., 1977.
7. D. F. Abell, *Defining the Business*, Prentice-Hall, Englewood Cliffs, N.J., 1980 gives a comprehensive survey of these problems.

# 6

# Competition

## Competitive advantage

Achievement of market strategies depends upon competitive advantage. If a business is able to operate more efficiently than its neighbours, it has freedom to decide its own strategies independently. It will be able more readily to use its array of weapons such as the opportunity to undercut the opposition in price, or to afford a better product quality, higher level of customer service, more sales personnel in the field or greater investment in new product research. These tactics inevitably lead to improved market share. The higher returns which were shown in Chapter 5 to result from such market position are, in fact, a consequence of competitive advantage.

Conversely, a business that does not enjoy competitive advantage is one that is unable to afford such actions and its strategies ultimately are only a reaction to what the more efficient are doing. Before considering the tactics that businesses may use to win success, however, the battlefield over which the competitive struggle will actually be waged has to be examined. What are the specific factors that are going to lead to competitive advantage?

A further revision of the diagram in Fig. 3.3 can be used again to illustrate the more important of these (see Fig. 6.1).

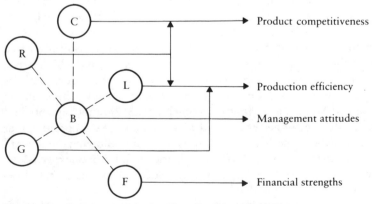

**Figure 6.1**  Business structure and competitive advantage

## Product competitiveness

The customer market is the most critical element: what products and services is the business offering and how do they compare with those provided by the competition? There are a wide variety of dimensions along which the comparison may be measured, including:

- price
- relative product quality and service
- the marketing effort
- the emphasis on research and innovation

### PRICE

Price is the most obvious weapon. Sell the same goods for less than the other company and the customers will flock in. Any experienced manager, however, knows that business is not like that. First, it is rare that products or services are identical to those offered by other companies and there is, therefore, some difficulty in judging which of those offered are the best buy in price terms. Anyone who has tried to calculate the relative prices of different packets of detergents in a supermarket knows the problem.

Second, even in the case of commodity products like detergents or decorative paints, considerable ingenuity is devoted to creating differences in the minds of customers. Thus Crown Paint introduced Matchpots, small samples of colour to try out on a wall before committing the customer to buy large quantities, while Dulux concentrated on producing new ranges of delicately tinted whites—very subtle differences which added significantly to value!

Third, even where there is no opportunity to differentiate on quality or price, there remain some options. Where the customer insists on a tight specification, other factors such as promotion become critical. If the product is sold in the consumer market, branding may be the answer, using advertising campaigns backed by product availability, point of sale material, distinctive packaging and so on. Indeed, by such means, premium prices can be obtained, even though there is little differentiation in the product itself.

Price is, in any event, an imperfect weapon as it is the most easily combated and the one to which the opposition can react most quickly.[1] In the high street, changes in Tesco's prices may be reflected in Gateway's within hours; perhaps not involving the same product lines, but overall giving an equivalent or better deal to customers. Major banks follow parallel interest rate movements in a matter of a day or two. Other goods and services may take longer. Popular daily newspapers hang on perhaps a week or two before following the upward lead of the first to change—though occasionally they indulge in unexpected behaviour as in the (temporary) 1p *drop* in the price of the Daily Mirror, following its acquisition by Robert Maxwell.

In most countries, anti-trust or fair trading legislation limits collusion, encouraging downward pressure on prices. On the downside of the trade cycle, there is normally a tactical drop in prices, as businesses attempt to retain volume. Once the competition has caught up, however, there is rarely any long-term advantage, and indeed, the fall in margins may be more or less permanent, as customers get used to and enjoy the benefits of lower supply costs. The only conditions under which undercutting can prove an effective weapon for gaining permanent market share is where the business has a sufficient cost advantage, or sufficient financial muscle to endure a sustained market war.

Market wars have varying lives, some may fizzle out after a few weeks, while others go on for ever. It is by no means certain that the business that precipitates a market war will win, not only because of the factors other than price which influence buyers' judgement, but also because of management attitudes, financial strength and other features that are considered later in this chapter. A well thought through campaign may be successful in gaining market share, but it is essential to know the enemy, and a strategy based upon price tactics alone is both risky and expensive.

QUALITY AND SERVICE

Research by the PIMS programme demonstrates clearly that more effective, though less dramatic ways of competing lie in providing better product quality and service than the opposition. Good service may be the only effective differentiation of one business from another. Steel stockholders and paper merchants have little opportunity to beat one another on quality. The ones who survive are those most responsive to customer needs and this often requires careful planning in partnership with the customer, to ensure that depots are properly located, specific grades are adequately stocked and transport is sufficiently available. One particular approach that a small supplier can very effectively use is to ensure a small position with a large number of big operator customers who wish to spread their exposure by making key purchases among a reasonably wide panel of suppliers.

Figure 6.2, taken from the PIMS programme, indicates the relationship between return on investment and relative product quality in the experience of the 2000 + companies on the PIMS data base.

Product quality and, equally, service are often difficult to measure in a quantified way. There will normally have to be a degree of judgement. Drugs may be assessed by their specific ability to cure a complaint, but fashion products are a matter of personal design preference and this is the important feature, given a satisfactory standard of materials and workmanship. In a magazine, the balance of editorial to advertising, the number of pages, the paper quality and the amount of colour may all be measured and give some guidance, but the quality of editorial can only be judged in the end by reference to the number of people who buy. Notwithstanding these problems of quantification, the chart in Fig. 6.2 clearly emphasizes the importance of making such judgements and

seeking competitive advantage in this dimension because of the strong leverage
that it has upon profitability.

MARKETING AND RESEARCH

Marketing effort refers principally to the expenditure devoted to the sales force
in the field and to promotion of all sorts. It is not true, however, that a vast
army of sales personnel and a high level of advertising is needed in every case.
Take a mature, orderly market producing high quality products, like the UK
legal books market. Excessive marketing effort of the nature described would
certainly not be cost effective. The competition has to be fought on quality and
service. It is in a fast growing market like that for electric showers in the late
'seventies in the UK, mentioned earlier, where it pays to get everyone out selling
and to adopt (within reason) a less stringent attitude to quality.

Research and innovation are also shown by PIMS to exert leverage on the
level of return on investment.[2] The results shown in Fig. 6.3 indicate that the
level of research and development with a view to bringing on new products (as
opposed to improving production techniques) and the percentage of sales derived from new products introduced in the last three years, are important. How
important depends necessarily on the other characteristics of the market. Some
constantly demand new, rather than renewed products. Pocket calculators are
an example of the former; children's comics of the latter type.

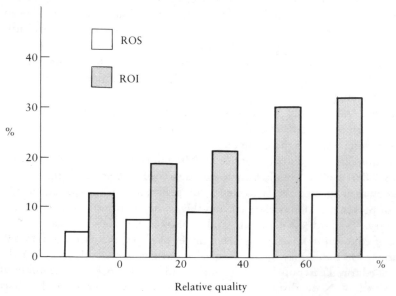

Figure 6.2   Higher returns through product quality

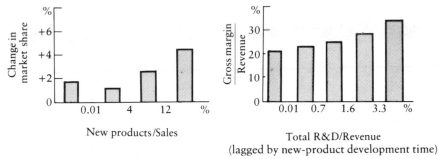

Figure 6.3  Raise share margins through research and innovation

## Production efficiency

This review of competitive advantage now moves to the production area. Lower costs and better quality clearly give an edge over the opposition and provide the freedom to decide and implement strategies ahead of the field. What are the means by which these advantages may be achieved? The first question to explore is productivity. Are Plinmo's employees, for example, producing as much value added as other manufacturers of plastic pipes?

There are as many ways of measuring productivity as there are analysts and the one to be chosen is entirely dependent on the dimension along which comparison is to be drawn, e.g.:

- total pipe produced *per capita*
- total pipe produced per man hour
- total pipe produced per unit raw materials/energy
- value added *per capita*
- total employment costs as a proportion of value added or sales

The last is the easiest to ascertain for UK companies as they are required by statute to report employee costs, as well as sales, in the annual report. It may be difficult to obtain figures on raw materials and bought-in services to get at value added, though some companies do publish value added data. The information in Fig. 6.4 was gleaned about Plinmo competitors by inspecting their published figures. Though the businesses all have some significant differences in product mix and type, the chart does give some guidance as to where Plinmo might have some advantages or otherwise, *vis-à-vis* the competition. In this case, Plinmo and competitor A are the low-cost labour users in the market.

APPLYING COMPETITIVE LEVERS

This leads to the next question: where can competitive levers be most successfully applied by Plinmo? The following, in addition to high relative market share, are the critical factors in achieving good productivity levels over a period of time:[3]

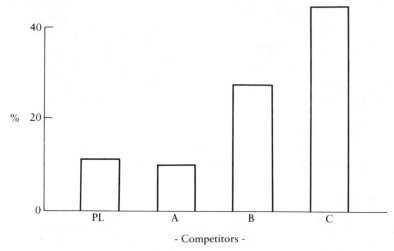

**Figure 6.4**   Employment costs/sales%

- rate of new product introduction
- the level of investment per employee
- the characteristic order size from customers
- relative product quality
- the level of R&D expenditure
- long-term real market growth
- percentage of employees unionized

The reason why most of these factors tend to improved productivity is evident from the earlier comments; those items that influence market share growth, such as higher investment, better product quality and greater research, will result in rising production volumes, as will high market growth. Higher investment should also improve efficiency of the equipment. Increased value added *per capita* should result. High levels of new product drag down productivity because of the learning curve involved. The order size is important because either a highly fragmented customer base or a very small number of customers tends to reduce productivity: more efficient levels lie in the intervening degrees of market fragmentation. The unionization point is important, not so much because of wage rates—often non-union houses pay more—but there is often a significantly higher manning level in a union plant and demarcations reduce the efficient use of labour.

Since the object of the exercise is to probe for advantage in a specific market sector, some of the above issues may be ignored. Thus, all operators in the market will enjoy the same long-term market growth and, normally, the same customer order size. This reduces the list to be investigated down to investment (automation), product quality, R&D and unionization. All are areas in which management action can have an impact.

NON-LABOUR EFFICIENCIES
Not all production efficiency, however, is dependent on the labour force. The following are also important issues, irrespective of the effective use of employees:

- runability of equipment
- output capacity
- quality and cost of raw materials
- rate of wastage
- integration between parts of the process

These are reasonably obvious and are not discussed further except that it should be pointed out that the last factor may refer at the small end of the scale to factory layout and at the large end to the integration of a process such as forestry, pulping and manufacture of newsprint in one locality. Where the competition is geographically placed (in North America or Scandinavia) to enable such full integration, it must have cost advantages over a UK business which has to import the pulp. In such a case, the UK mill has to search for some way to get round this disadvantage. One solution has been to use waste materials, though the cost of such materials remains susceptible to dollar pulp prices and hence exchange rates.

Not all operating efficiencies are production efficiencies. In most businesses, many other areas will also allow advantage, including:

- warehousing and distribution
- sales and marketing
- advertising and promotion
- administration

As for all other parts of the business, these functions should be reviewed so that wherever feasible, significant opportunities to get some advantage over the competition may be pursued.

## Management capability

Certain aspects of management are also important in this context. Faced with determined competition, will they fight, retreat, know how to cope, be ruthless, persistent, or what? A judgement on these characteristics may be as important as knowing the weak points in the product offering or production facility.

An interesting feature of private companies, or those with very dominant chief executives who command a substantial block of votes, is that they may be able to adopt strategies and tactics that the boards of public companies, answerable to the body of shareholders, would be unwilling to risk. Pilkington, the glass manufacturers, devoted a very large resource and many years' research to the development of its float glass process. As a result of success, it established a clear technological lead. Without the dedication of the Pilkington family who controlled the business and their agreement to spending so much time and money on what may have seemed like an impossible dream at times, it would never have happened. The pay-off would have been too remote and risky for institutional investors.

Individual owners may operate in a way which could be described as either visionary or idiosyncratic, according to the cynicism of the commentator. It has to be admitted, however, that so-called professional managers can also act in an individualistic way. If business success has been built over time on the back of a particular product which is now failing, it is likely that management effort and money will go on being applied in trying to keep that business alive long after life support should have been cut.

There are other ailments, too, that affect executives, such as 'acquisition fever'. Having started bidding at a rational level, the fever grips the Board and the sufferers have to continue bidding until they buy, whatever the cost. Then there is the 'plant bug', whose symptoms are continually adding to plant capacity, whatever the state of long-term demand in the market. The point is that all businesses are run by people who have their own fads and foibles and it will surely repay managers to study how the individuals against whom they are pitting themselves in the market place respond to challenges. It can be as critical in assessing where competitive advantage lies as any other feature of business.

## Financial strengths

A further important business characteristic in assessing the opposition is its financial strength. A small business like Plinmo, if it were competing with one of Conglom's subsidiaries, would know that it could not force Conglom through shortage of funds to give up its market position. There may be other reasons why Conglom might throw in the towel, but its financial strength would enable it to keep going far longer against competitive pressures than could Plinmo.

Pointers to the financial importance of a business to its owners which have to be taken into account when deciding whether to attack a competitor's share include:

- Size of investment: does it represent a major part of the enemy's business into which they are likely to pile more resource in defence of their position?
- Duration of investment: not only the question of whether the competitor has been involved in the sector for a long time, but also, whether it is a new activity which is being pursued with vigour;

- Vertical integration: is the activity closely tied up with any other part of the competitor's business which would be adversely affected by its disposal or closure—or even just by diminishing its market share?
- Write-off: would the termination of a business result in a very high, even catastrophic write-off? It is an understandable, though unacceptable fact of corporate life that even though assets may have lost their value through losing their profit generating capacity, many managements will not write them down until forced to do so by some triggering event such as closure. They build up a great log-jam of lost value which they become increasingly unable to deal with in the ordinary course of business.

Again, all of these issues are of significance in coming to a view about how readily competitive advantage may be wrested from the opposition. Taken as a whole the market place and the features of competition are very complex. Ways in which the information on them may be sifted and manipulated are discussed in Chapters 12 and 13.


### The composition of the competition

One particular technique that assists in this, i.e. market audit, however, is considered here because it raises a further question; what does the competition actually comprise? It is a common fault when looking at a market place to ignore the likelihood of change in the competition from causes other than those induced by the proposed actions of the business. There are two possibilities:

- new competition may come in and old campaigners may depart;
- the structure of the market may change from protected, monopolistic, orderly, fragmented, etc. to some other of these states.

The reason for such changes may be new technology; an invention, an improved process, a substitute product may come in to replace existing goods and services, or the way in which they are manufactured or provided. Had Plinmo been in business 20 years ago, it might have been making glazed earthenware, cast-iron or pitch fibre pipes. The impact on its activities of the newfangled plastics would have been devastating if it had not seen the threat coming down the road and acted accordingly.

A temporary, or even permanent change in the alignment of exchange rates could be another cause. Sterling strengthened to a new, though fluctuating level, as a result of its oil-based status. This followed the exploitation of the North Sea oil and gas reserves. As a result, during periods of high energy prices, sterling tends to rise against other currencies and imports come flooding in. At present, with weak oil prices, the pound has fallen. Holland has a similar currency status, but has a more controlled economy. In consequence this has tended to make Dutch manufacture less competitive and has accelerated the opening of their markets to foreign (particularly German) competition, though its low inflation both in prices and wage rates counteracts this to a degree.

Changes in structure may also be precipitated by new foreign sellers penetrating the national scene. UK carton manufacturers enjoyed an orderly market for many years until the Scandinavians and others started to arrive from the mid-'seventies. Less directly, corrugated case makers had a relatively protected market until those to whom they sold, and especially white goods manufacturers started to suffer severely from imports—Italian refrigerators and washing machines were not packed in British boxes. Both carton and case makers have suffered reduced market advantage, therefore, though for different reasons.

Even monopoly situations can be eroded by these sorts of influences. The development of broadcasting technology over the last 30 years has meant that TV and radio stations have been able to break the advertising monopoly formerly enjoyed in specific localities by the local press.

Uninvited guests may invade the market place: it is also possible that some competitors will move out unexpectedly. A business may have over-extended itself and needs to streamline into fewer market sectors; it may be making excessive losses. Whatever the reason, there will be clues that are worth following to come to a view of the effect this will have on market share.


### Market audit

In considering the whole competitive position, therefore, it is important to contemplate the potential as well as the existing suppliers in the field. As indicated, a useful technique for appraising this systematically is market audit. A careful review of each market sector is required against the following (or similar) headings:

- market growth rate
- product life cycle
- vulnerability to substitute technology of product or production
- changes in domestic competition
- changes in foreign competition
- market structure

The market growth rate will tend to set the scene for the market tactics: if it is fast growing, the sort of approach to quality and marketing effort will be as described earlier; if the market is static, different tactics are needed. The life cycle phase describes this same feature from a different angle. For this discussion, the cycle may be usefully divided into five phases (though there is nothing sacrosanct about this classification):

- *Introductory*   The potential customers are just becoming aware of the available product (e.g. personal computers in the UK, 1982); growth is low and there is a large offering in new designs;

- *High growth*    The market is now aware of what is available and growth takes off, starting with those who have an immediate need for the product, but soon proliferating into a large number of 'me too' customers (e.g. personal computers in 1984); design starts to stabilize and market leaders begin to emerge;
- *Moderate growth*    The 'followers' who do not have an immediate use now buy, the competition is beginning to settle into market niches with clearly defined product;
- *Maturity*    Growth slows down and tops out; the product is beginning to be viewed more as a commodity; price competition becomes more common (e.g. decorative paint);
- *Decline*    There is a generally slow reduction in demand for the product, competition intensifies as overcapacity problems become increasingly acute and weak suppliers are ousted from the market (e.g. wallcoverings).

The likely future development of the market and whether it is an area to

**Table 6.1**    Market audit, Plinmo Limited October 1979—Product: plastic pipes/mouldings

| Factor | Time | Impact |
|---|---|---|
| Market growth: | Now | 5% pa. |
| | 5 years hence | 2% pa. |
| Life cycle phase | Now | Moderate growth |
| | 5 years hence | Mature |
| Vulnerability to | New technology | |
| | Probability | 20% |
| | Impact | 20% loss of share |
| | Domestic competition | |
| | Probability | 80% |
| | Impact | 10% loss of share |
| | Foreign competition | |
| | Probability | 60% |
| | Impact | 10% loss of share |
| Market structure | Now | Orderly |
| | 5 years hence | Fragmented |

*Notes*
Market growth is volume growth of the total market.
Vulnerability factors do not differentiate between substituted product and production techniques; if either were a significant factor, it may be shown separately.
Competition refers to new and not existing competition.

contemplate reinforcing or reducing may be deduced from this. The other features of the audit have been discussed earlier.

MARKET AUDIT FOR PLINMO

Plinmo might have used this procedure to produce the results in Table 6.1 about five years ago: this out-of-date analysis is used as it is so much easier to be wise after the event!

The picture the table gives is of a fast maturing market. The expectation of new domestic competition in this market, had Plinmo been a real business, would have been fulfilled. The actual operators in the UK such as Marley, Key Terrain and IMI have felt the impact of the new and vigorous competitor, Polypipe. Equally, such a situation coupled with a price cutting policy on the part of a major continental operator has quickly changed the market from its previously orderly state.

With this type of market audit, backed by a detailed assessment of both present and prospective competitive advantage, Plinmo is in a position to specify the particular business tactics it is going to use to achieve its market strategies. This is, to a degree, a counsel of perfection. Businesses do get by with a far less analytical approach. Nevertheless, careful planning of the sort outlined will, in itself, help to give any business a competitive advantage of its own and those who can discard part of the process are those who have been through it and know what is critical and what is not.

## Notes

1. M. E. Porter, *Competitive Strategy*, Free Press, New York, 1980.
2. D. W. Collier *et al.*, 'How effective is technological innovation?', *Research Management* vol. 27, no. 5, September/October 1984, pp. 11–16.
3. B. T. Gale, 'Can more capital buy higher productivity?', *Harvard Business Review* vol. 58, no. 4, July/August 1980, pp. 78–86.

# 7

# Business tactics

## The nature of tactics

Objectives have been set and the market strategies, with their attendant goals, worked out. Management has carefully studied the competitive environment and is now ready to start planning in detail what it is going to do to achieve those goals. At last this is beginning to get nearer to the real action, where live bullets crack through the air. It is moving away from the rarified atmosphere of the long-term direction of the business. As a result, the tactics to be chosen are inherently of a shorter time-scale and may be treated with much less respect than a strategy. If a tactic does not work, try another—though not capriciously and not without a real effort in seeking to implement it.

The tactics to be used will be a mixture of actions designed to achieve competitive advantage (where the strategy is to increase or maintain market share) and actions to increase or decrease investment.[1] These are structured for consideration into the following categories (the first two of which are certainly familiar):

- product offer
- production efficiency
- organization and overhead
- growing the business
- diminishing the investment base

## Product offer

One of the first issues confronting any manager launching a new product is what price is to be charged. The dangers of price cutting have been examined earlier, but it is common for a new product to go into the market at a lower price than will be charged once it has asserted its presence. From then on, the manager has to be constantly assessing the price/volume balance. As a general rule, the higher the price charged, the lower the volume sold, though all sorts of other factors modify this rule, such as the need for the product, or availability of alternatives.

One way of manipulating volume without upsetting the price balance in the market place is to change the quality of the product offered. Sales managers are, of course, changing mix every day of their lives as they wheel and deal in the market place. What is to be considered here, however, is a major, deliberate move to improve or reduce quality in order to go for a richer or cheaper segment of the market. Either tactic may be a response to severe competition: a move upwards could be to get out of the uncomfortably unprofitable mass sector; a move downwards may be made to cut costs and to enable the business to meet price competition.

A further option is to broaden the product base, either by adding additional lines or by offering reinforcing services such as consultancy, delivery, or financing. A microcomputer manufacturer would certainly add services to help customers to use the equipment most effectively; new software packages might be provided, together with hardware maintenance and computer consumables such as tapes, floppy discs and the like. The converse of diminishing the offer requires a reduced number of lines or the withdrawal of ancillary services.

Suppose that Plinmo (which is clearly not a market leader) has looked at competitive plastic pipe products and perceived that the opposition is undercutting on price. It is not in a position to sustain a prolonged market war, but management, for all the sorts of reasons given before, has determined that it wishes to maintain market share. Well aware of the unproductive pain of a price battle, is its response, nevertheless, to be to follow suit, or will it prefer to sit the attack out, relying on quality and service, even though some and perhaps a large piece of the market will be lost to the opposition before the market settles down again? The one thing it cannot afford to do is to adopt a passive stance. The options Plinmo has in terms of product offer include:

- price with the opposition and do nothing more;
- put more sales people in the field and strengthen customer service and the network of contacts;
- move upmarket into higher value added moulded products with which to hold volume of commodity type extruded pipe products (though some margin on this may have to be sacrificed);
- broaden the range of pipe size and mouldings offered to get more out of the market; increasing the breadth of the offer is often as effective as trying to sell more of the same in wresting market share from the opposition;
- bring new products to the market place to compete effectively with the existing—perhaps lighter-weight, longer-life or easier-to-fix substitutes.

All may be valid options given differing competitive environments and the different strategies chosen. It is better that Jack Robinson should plan in advance what he intends to do than to leave it to instant reactions in the market place.

## Production efficiency

On the question of actions to reduce costs, the productivity issue discussed earlier has been in the forefront of any discussion on the UK national economy for some time. Regrettably, the proportion of value added paid out in employment costs in the UK generally remains higher than the most efficient of the foreign competitors, the Germans and Japanese. There is little that can be done immediately to change this situation except at the macroeconomic level by allowing the exchange rate to fall. It will be a long war of attrition to reduce expectations of wage increases in this country to the level of those of the strongest competition.

Against domestic competitors, however, where all are working within the same constraints, the situation is different. Much is now being done to reduce overmanning. In some areas, confrontation with the Unions to force through reduced manning levels is regrettably the only way. In others a more enlightened joint approach is proving a more effective route. The electrical and engineering unions are nowadays taking a particularly positive stance.

Apart from the direct approach to employment costs, there are two further tactics to enhance operating efficiencies:

- automation
- vertical integration

Automation is a favourite ploy at present—and not just on the shop floor. The availability of word processors, microcomputers and other information manipulation devices can make possible substantial changes in the way in which the office and indeed the whole marketing function can work. Friends Provident, the life assurance company, automated its offices a few years ago and, as a consequence, were able to move a substantial amount of responsibility for approving risks to local branch managers and put the back office staff who typed out the policies into direct contact with customers; reduced controls meant fewer delays so that a new client could walk in off the street and out of the shop again clutching a policy. As a result of this streamlining, the much improved customer service resulted in soaring sales volumes.

THE DANGERS OF AUTOMATION

Automation, none the less, is not a universal cure. There are many situations in which it may be counter-productive to invest in further equipment. It has been demonstrated that the following business characteristics do not, as a general rule, combine well with high investment per employee (which is taken as an indicator of the level of automation).[2]

- high rate of product innovation
- low capacity utilization
- market decline

The reason for these mismatches is self-evident. It is difficult to keep pace with new products in mechanization terms and if utilization of plant is low and reducing through market decline, there is little point in adding to the investment. Nevertheless, none of these generalizations is sacrosanct. They only point to results which will follow unless there is some special situation.

Another general assertion is that those with a low market share get less benefit from automation than do those with high market share. However, not to seek ultimately to improve market share through any rational cost-cutting means is a policy of despair. Tactics designed to raise share by automation with consequent price, quality or supply advantage, particularly where a competitor is not looking to do likewise, could pay off handsomely.

The real danger is the mechanization trap. A business may introduce new technology to cut the labour force. The depreciation charges for the additional plant, plus added spares and maintenance costs and the expense of running-in could represent a substantial element in the equation. If the labour cost savings (offset by severance or redundancy payments to employees rendered surplus to the requirements of the particular operation) are not greater than the additional costs of mechanization, the whole exercise will prove to have been a trap. Managers should resist the engineers who seek to draw them into it in the interests of excellence rather than commercial expediency.

Not that it was engineers who created the débâcles in Fleet Street in the 'seventies. National newspaper publishers, seeking to emulate the successful introduction of technology in Japan, for example at the Asai Shimbun, or in the smaller regional presses in the United States, used new automatic page composition systems as an attempt to break through the excessive labour cost barrier. As a general rule they failed and were left both with the equipment (admittedly most of which they were allowed by the unions to introduce), and with even higher labour costs as a proportion of sales than before. Times have, nevertheless, now changed!

VERTICAL INTEGRATION
Vertical integration is the move upstream towards primary manufacture, extraction or harvesting, or downstream closer to the ultimate customer. For Plinmo, upstream would mean getting into PVC manufacture and at the remotest level, oil exploration. Downstream it would involve getting into a builders' merchant or even a jobbing plumbing business. The objective is to take a greater part of the value added out of the market and increase profitability by applying know-how and common services and management to an operation. The easiest measure of vertical integration is the level of value added retained by a business; the higher this is compared to industry peers, the more likely that the business is more highly integrated with suppliers and/or customers than its neighbours.

Again, there are dangers in this approach. Each stage of the processing chain has to be adequately profitable in its own right, otherwise it acts as a drain on the whole. If the manufacture of PVC requires heavy capital investment, both in equipment and inventories, the cash flow costs of this may far outweigh the benefits of adding the profit from this stage of the process.

There are, nevertheless, a number of situations in which vertical integration becomes highly desirable.

- Shortage of supplies: there may be a need to ensure that the business gets enough of its raw materials to make its planned production volumes. In the 'fifties, newspaper publishers held interests in newsprint manufacturers when, following the end of rationing, there was not just a fear but a reality of shortages. By having a secure supply, not only was the owner's business not starved of raw materials, but it was certainly possible from time to time that the opposition had problems. At the least this was likely to mean higher prices or lower quality for them.
- Tight specification on materials: it may be necessary to get control of the supplier if quality is critical and needs careful control.
- Other operational reasons may demand integration: such as, for instance (and again using Fleet Street as the example), a national daily newspaper and its printing; here, the changes in page make-up during the night and every night, make it essential for the publisher to control the operation; a magazine publisher or local newspaper proprietor does not have the same need to own a printery, and indeed the disadvantages of doing so, because its capital intensity and the need to maintain full working to maximize profitability, may prove decisive.

*The problems of vertical integration*
This last comment points to the dangers inherent in going for a further share of the value added in the market by moving downstream. It may be desirable for the oil company or the brewer to tie in petrol filling stations or public houses; certainly petrol and, alas, beer, are commodities and a satisfactorily wide range of their own product can be offered by the manufacturers in such tied establishments. It would, however, be a mad grocer who chose to buy a supermarket to stock it only with the goods that he manufactured. Plinmo could not in prudence, buy a builders' merchants and constrain it only to sell plastic pipes. It could, however, sell all the normal range of building products produced by other manufacturers, limiting only pipe sales to its own. That might make sense.

The magazine publisher mentioned above does not have a similar freedom. It might not allow its printer to work on a closely competing publication and it is even more unlikely that such a competitor would want to put himself in the hands of his rival in any way. The notice by Associated Newspapers to terminate the printing of the colour supplement to the *Mail on Sunday* by Robert Maxwell's BPCC printing concern because of Maxwell's association with Mirror Group Newspapers, is a good example. As a result, the printers cannot operate freely to maximize their return on investment. Unless publishers who own a printery can continuously fill it with work, they cannot afford to make an investment of this nature.

A practical problem that normally arises upon vertical integration as a result of conflicting interests of the upstream and downstream businesses, is that ultimately one of such businesses achieves ascendancy and tends to make a profit at the expense of the other. All the wrangles that go on in groups about inter-company prices are a symptom of this problem. The forerunner of BPCC mentioned above, was dominantly a printer and made more of a success out of that side of the business than from its publishing, whereas International Publishing Corporation was precisely the opposite—and its printing was, in practice, a service for the benefit of its publishers.

It is also true that substantial differences in management style may make a business up or downstream very difficult to run. Any manufacturer who has tried without previous successful experience to get into retailing will recount horror stories of such an attempt. The selling mechanism is different—not through a string of sales people in the field, but by assistants behind counters; alternative measurements of success or failure apply—perhaps a supermarket that can make a five per cent net margin on sales is doing very well while this could mean substantial losses for a manufacturer. The whole culture is different and this has to be taken into account. Vertical integration, selectively used, may be a profitable venture, but it has its major pitfalls.

### Organization and overhead

The structure of a business can have an impact upon profitability. It is commonly thought that size will give benefits. It is assumed that overhead can be spread. As a general rule, the benefits of scale only hold good within a specific market sector. This results from the profit impact of high market share. Once the business straddles a number of markets, the beneficial effect may soon be dissipated as the larger organization becomes the target for union activity, lax management practice and the inevitable drift to lusher corporate benefits—not least to attract good people who might be prepared to tolerate more spartan living were they working for themselves.

Thus an organization such as Conglom, if it has a dominant position in a number of separate markets, is likely as a result of that factor, to be able to achieve good profits at the activity level. These then are in danger of being diluted by an excessive overhead. It is a feature of management in the recent somewhat straitened times that many large corporations have reduced substantially their headquarters staff; ICI is a good example. The question that has to be asked is why it was necessary in any event to extend the central staffing in the past, if the company can now operate successfully without them.

SPECIFIC COST REDUCTION LEVERS

Leaving aside until Part 2 the detailed discussion of the structure of an organization, there are a number of specific levers that can be pulled in this area to reduce costs. These include:

- white collar productivity
- accommodation
- house services

The first has been considered above under the heading 'Production efficiency'. The second represents the opportunity to accommodate the business at an economic cost, both in rent and rates. The move of many companies out of the centre of London is a symptom of this. One problem, however, is the very high cost of removal, including severance pay for people who are unwilling or unable to move and the cost (and difficulty) of recruitment and training of new staff. The question of house services often involves consideration of the need to provide the service internally at all. Some departments could be replaced by external consultants, such as legal, share registration, catering or cleaning. Decision on which is the more cost effective route is more likely to affect the large business—bosses of small firms will be bound to go outside for their lawyers but for other services they and their staff may very well turn their own hands to the task.

## Growing the business

The growth of a business organically, by increasing market penetration through the various product offer and production efficiency routes has been considered above. Growth by acquisition or by 'greenfields' ventures are also treated earlier, but as part of strategic rather than tactical options. In practice, such actions have often to be linked as alternatives: for example the guideline could be acquire, but if this fails go for greenfields development. Furthermore, to have nominated the acquisition of a particular business as the strategy to be followed is unrealistic: such strategy may be readily defeated by the rejection of the bid or by the demand for too high a price. In consequence, if the strategy indicates generally a preference to buy rather than develop into a market, the tactics will nominate a number of specific candidates for investigation and specify whether to go for one major acquisition or to put together a jigsaw puzzle of smaller pieces, or even to acquire one small one with the intention of using it as the nucleus round which to grow the business.

One tactical opportunity in planning a greenfields venture is the location of the production unit. The tendency is to put it alongside existing plant, if there is room on the site. The assumption is that the contribution to overhead is the main cost saving benefit to go for. This may be short-sighted and good

Table 7.1    Investment failure rates

| Type of venture | Failure rate % |
| --- | --- |
| Greenfields | 17 |
| Direct acquisition | 30 |
| Indirect acquisition | 38 |

managements will consider other advantages to be gained from an alternative siting, including:

- favourable government grants or tax treatment
- cheaper available labour
- closer access to markets or (rarely) raw material supplies

Most of such investigations stop short of crossing the Channel, let alone the Atlantic or other ocean. This commercial hydrophobia precludes any adequate review of sourcing in areas where there may be very significant advantages of the nature described. Certainly there will be problems of dealing in a new language and a new culture which are formidable, but knowing the enormous productivity benefits which competitors operating out of such areas may enjoy, it must be sensible to contemplate sharing the competitors' advantage. The alternative is to fail, with a UK cost base, to match the keen pricing which the overseas manufacturers are able to apply when importing into Britain. It may be possible to achieve the objective by contract rather than investment in fixed assets and a work force. The important point is to be prepared to search for any such opportunity.

FAILURE OF INVESTMENT

Reasons for failure in overseas investment have been extensively analysed.[3] Curiously no similarly focused research has been carried out for the domestic market, but the conclusions of the study seem from experience to be applicable there, too, though the percentages may be somewhat different. Broadly, the message is that the failure rate for greenfields ventures is about half that for acquisitions and that a business acquired as part of a larger takeover fails more often than a business directly purchased for its own potential. The percentage failure rates shown by the study referred to are given in Table 7.1.

Other lessons that can be learnt from the study of interest in tactical planning are these:

- do not at any one time move too quickly, or in too many different sectors, away from areas in which the business is experienced;
- keep a balance among the businesses so that the biggest does not overwhelm the rest and the rest are not a proliferation of small activities;

- time the expansion to minimize the balance and diversity problems outlined above.

This has been translated into the following specific steps:

- add a single new activity of small relative size;
- build on this new activity and add a second, relatively small, new activity;
- build on new activities one and two and add relatively small, new activity three;
- and so on ...

This sounds like common sense, but it is remarkable from the evidence of the performance of 69 of the largest continental European multinationals that a large number of them did not appear to follow this pattern. The point about this careful step-by-step approach is that it avoids hurling small units of troops onto the spears of the Goths and the Gauls in all-out attacks across a broad front; it enables managers overseeing the programme to focus efforts and learn as they go. Furthermore, if the new businesses are in markets closely allied to existing operations, the learning process is shorter.

It is often assumed that experience in production is the key to success. In fact, it is knowledge of the market that is more important. In almost all cases, production know-how can be bought in and applied more readily within the business than can market know-how. It is for this reason that the common, but dangerous philosophy of planning to increase capacity utilization by selling into new markets is suspect, and when capacity is actually increased because the production team knows all there is to know about the product, the trouble can really start. Sometimes it can be done, but genius and/or luck are not a safe basis for planning.

## Reducing the assumed investment

Just as flexibility is needed for growth strategies, so is it also desirable in respect of strategies to reduce the investment. This is particularly true where the business is plainly on a downward trend and retrenchment is forced upon management. There is little point in insisting on disposal or merely cut-back, when ultimately, there has to be total closure. On the other hand, to demand that a closure strategy be followed when a good offer has been received for a business is quixotic, unless there is a consequential danger of exposing a flank (by opening up an opportunity to a competitor). It is only where a harvest strategy is an unforced choice, perhaps to release investment for another market sector, that the proposed manner of implementation may be strictly adhered to.

One problem facing any management in a situation of diminishing demand and intensifying competition is the speed at which a strategy for moving out of the market should be pursued. Proper concern for the staff who may have

**Table 7.2**    Plinmo tactical summary

| Sector | Tactic | Target | Date* |
|---|---|---|---|
| Food containers | Reduce staff by introducing new plant | Purchase machine A | 1/2/85 |
| | | Transfer 2 operators to maintenance | 1/4/85 |
| | | Take 3 volunteers (or nominate) for redundancy | 1/4/85 |
| | Improve cost base and quality and hold price | Reduce unit labour costs by 7% | 1/12/85 |
| | | Switch to new supplier | 1/7/85 |
| Plastic pipes | Reduce price on pipe | Price reduction 5% | 1/1/85 |
| | Introduce new product line at higher value added | Hire 2 new salesmen | 1/2/85 |
| | | Launch product | 1/3/85 |
| | | Achieve gross margin of 45% | ongoing |
| | Move into export market | Hire selling agent in Gulf | 1/5/85 |
| | | Sell 10 000 pieces | 1/1/86 |
| Motor accessories | Reduce product line | Cease production on all but three best sellers | 1/2/85 |
| | | Cut total inventory by 50% | 1/7/85 |
| | Increase prices | Prices on remaining lines up by average 20% | 1/3/85 |
| | Cut sales force | Retrain 2 salesmen for new business | 1/12/85 |
| | Make offers for Natplast Ltd† | Maximum price £2.5m | 1/6/85 |
| | Carlink Ltd† | Maximum price £1.4m | 1/7/85 |
| | | Finalise contracts | 1/10/85 |
| | | Complete | 1/12/85 |
| | | Transfer retrained salesmen | 1/1/86 |

*Final date to complete action    †Alternative proposals

worked there a lifetime and as efficiently as plant and management allowed, often results in a prolonged withdrawal in an attempt to minimize damage. There are, nevertheless, other considerations. A business in the hands of the managers as owners, or merged with another, so that together they enjoy a good market share, may become viable in the new context. These superior solutions are often blocked off because they are not adopted in time—the business gets too run down for such creative options to be realistic. Thus the business, with all the people involved, dies a death of a thousand cuts when early amputation might have saved its life and the jobs of many of the work-force. The basic message is that even in an inevitable realization, a timely approach to the divestment strategy will afford an opportunity to apply a wider variety of effective tactics.

## Setting targets

The foregoing has set out briefly the main tactical options. The tactics chosen should be quantified as targets. The targets specify in detail how a tactic is to be achieved in much the same way as goals are a means to specify strategies. The targets also provide a most effective means of monitoring business performance. Table 7.2 outlines a sample set for Plinmo. These tactics follow from the strategies and goals set out in Chapter 5. Note that a reasonably precise timing is projected.

The plan can only be a skeleton; it should include details of sales volumes, prices, key production parameters, wage rate increases, unit labour and raw material costs and so on. None the less, it indicates broadly the structure of the tactical plan and how it is derived from the strategies. One thing at least is clear. Having gone through the whole process in this way the plan provides a succinct but complete working document, without the need for a lot of words. An important element is missing, however. That is the element of surprise, and it is this which is addressed in the next chapter.

## Notes

1. For this topic generally, see M. E. Porter, *Competitive Strategy*, Free Press, New York, 1980.
2. B. T. Gale, 'Can more capital buy higher productivity?', *Harvard Business Review*, July/August 1980, pp. 78–86.
3. W. T. Bane and F. F. Neubauer, 'Diversification, the failure of new foreigh activities', *Strategic Management Journal* vol. 2, 1981, pp. 219–233.

# 8

# The turbulent environment

## The purpose of forecasting

There are few people nowadays who believe in a bunch of gods living on Olympus and toying with mortals for their sport. Yet the explanatory power of this concept may on occasions seem to be better than that of some econometric models of the world. Over 10 years ago, the London *Economist* rebuked forecasters as 'All the false prophets'.[1] World food production, levels of raw material supplies, and the pace of technological development were all areas in which certain well-publicized predictions had not merely got it wrong, but had failed to say anything meaningful at all!

Inept forecasters have a lot to answer for: they brought what is a perfectly sensible and necessary approach into some disrepute. And it is fruitless for them to plead that nobody reads the small print. Despite the qualifications with which they hedge round their predictions, the flaws remain. The debate comes down to this: are the projections of econometricians and other commentators any improvement on the assumption that all events should be treated as unique and random? The answer must be a qualified 'yes'. All humans build up in their own minds a picture of the world in which they live. They use their experience to tell them that certain structures exist, in the social world as well as in the physical.

The London Underground is such a system. It combines a human organization with a physical structure (tunnels, rails, rolling stock, etc.). If a man wishes to travel from King's Cross to Victoria, there are many routes he may follow, but the quickest (normally) is via the Victoria line. He knows that if he turns up at King's Cross at 8 a.m. on a Monday morning, he may reasonably expect trains to be running at regular intervals, but if there is a fire at Oxford Circus station, he will still be able to get to his destination in some other way. A foreknowledge of the system makes it easier to use effectively.

In the same way, knowledge of the structure of the larger socio-economic system in which businesses operate must be able to provide some clues for future behaviour, even though it may only be possible to hazard guesses at times as to the timing and direction of the economic and political forces within it.

The difference between these forces and those deriving from the immediate market in which the business is operating (as described in Chapter 6) is their scale. They go right across the national and even global scene and yet can have immediate and devastating effect upon the individual business. They cannot normally be detected by keeping an eye only upon the individual market trends; they have to be watched at the macro level.

The case of oil prices particularly illustrates the way in which these macro-economic factors can have an impact right across the frontiers of business sectors and cost categories—and without much warning. So Plinmo, in the wake of the 1974 oil price rises would have first felt their influence upon raw material prices and upon shortages, since PVC is a petroleum-based product. Little immediate impact would have been felt from the rise in energy costs, as Plinmo is a relatively low energy consumer. In due course, however, the greatest effect would have come from the way in which oil prices affected demand. In many developed countries, liquidity crises, massive inflation and soaring interest rates, all directly stemming from the oil price hike, resulted in substantially falling demand, including in Plinmo's area, the construction sector. On the other hand, demand in the underdeveloped OPEC states boomed. The Gulf, Saudi Arabia and Nigeria became very favoured markets for pipe extruders like Plinmo.

### Listing the influences

It is evident from a review of these influences on Plinmo that there are a number of areas that would repay study. It is worth trying to draw up a full list for any business of those factors which seem to be critical. Obviously it will not be possible to identify all future influences, but this approach makes a useful start. A modified Fig. 3.3 diagram introduces the analysis for Plinmo in Fig. 8.1. The points at which changes in these factors influence the business cash flow are shown in the tree in Fig. 8.2.

In practice, the manager of a small business has time only to be aware of

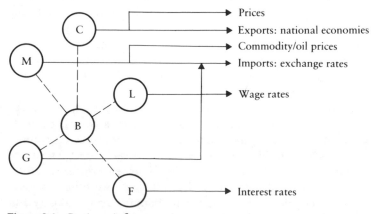

**Figure 8.1** Business influences

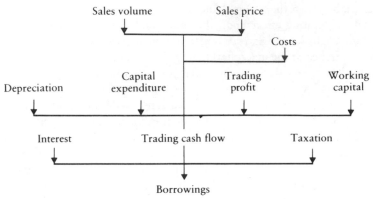

**Figure 8.2**    Pressure points on cash flow

these items and cannot delve into a great deal of detail. Nevertheless, there is a pay-off in understanding the basic cause/effect arguments. Certainly, any executives who are involved in running a number of different businesses, where they cannot rely fully upon personal experience, will need to do so. The following discussion seeks to describe some of the more important aspects of the economic environment and how it is possible to construct an adequate system to review what is going on.

## Inflation

Perhaps the most important feature over the past decade has been inflation. Inflation is the increase in price for goods or services (including labour) without any increase in value. It reduces the purchasing power of money.[2] Plinmo may sell an identical moulding in 1983 for £8 and in 1984 for £9. This represents a 12.5 per cent increase. This is inflation. Equally, it may produce a moulding for the same price, made from lower quality materials. This change may also be called inflationary and, if the product performs in an inferior way—for example by fracturing more frequently—it certainly is. On the other hand a £9 moulding that performs substantially better than the model it replaces is not inflationary to the extent that it offers improved value.

Inflation is customarily publicized in national statistics through the retail price index (RPI). This is an index built up from price data covering a wide variety of goods and services. They include food, clothing, transport, consumer durables like cookers and fridges and even the mortgage rate.[3] The price changes are weighted according to the relative importance of the expenditure items within the economy. In addition to the RPI there are other national indices like the producer price index (PPI) for all manufacturing industry and other sectoral data such as the PPI for metal windows and doors.[4]

Among the adverse consequences of inflation is its effect upon cash flow and the distortion of the information that can be gained from traditional methods of accounting. Big increases in the costs of raw materials and in the replacement cost of equipment means that profits and the value of plant and equipment are overstated in the accounts. So-called stock profits make the figures look better than they are, as does an inadequate provision for depreciation. Cash is not being generated at the rate which these figures, in a low inflation environment, imply. These effects were fully discussed some time ago in the Sandilands Report.[5] Current cost accounting (CCA)[6] was a proposed solution which, very simply, required stocks, plant and buildings to be valued at current cost, as well as making adjustments in monetary items (debtors, creditors, borrowings, etc.) in view of their loss in value. Because of the substantial abatement in inflation, however, such an approach is no longer considered useful, though it may well be resurrected should we again suffer the runaway inflation rates of the 'seventies.

## The base-case

A more useful approach enables the impact of inflation and many other factors to be assessed on the plans of a business through scenario planning. This requires a review of the influence of changes in the key assumptions on which the plans are based. These alternative assumptions about the future are called scenarios.[7]

Before getting involved in alternative scenarios, however, a business has to establish for itself the key assumptions about the environment upon which it is going to prepare its plans. These assumptions, called the 'base-case', are like any other set of scenario assumptions, except that they represent the most likely future in the mind of the forecaster at the time the predictions are made.

The amount of detail required to be considered for the base-case is reasonably limited. So long as the business has gone through the process of listing the important issues and knowing how sensitive it is to changes in them, it need not involve itself in any other numbers. Table 8.1 gives illustrations of some of the critical parameters used in a previous year for Plinmo's plan.

These assumptions have to be consistent with one another. This means that the forecasts have to be derived from a single model that has been reasonably well tested and seems to give adequate results. What cannot be done is to pick and choose the assumptions from a number of different sources. That would be meaningless, even if by chance the variables were subsequently all proved right!

From the practical point of view, this normally means that the business will use as the basis for its plans the projections made by some reputable forecasting agency.[8] Only very large corporations who have special needs will build their own macro-model. The choice of which agency to use will depend on their track record regarding the variables that are important for the business.

**Table 8.1**   Planning assumptions

|  | % change yearly in value | Year 1 | 2 | 3 |
|---|---|---|---|---|
| Markets: | New housing—public | − 14.5 | + 6.0 | + 5.5 |
|  | —private | + 11.0 | + 6.0 | + 3.0 |
|  | Other new construction work | + 1.5 | − 0.5 | + 0.5 |
|  | Repairs, renovations | − 1.0 | + 10.0 | + 3.0 |
| Costs: | Polymer prices | + 25.0 | + 19.7 | + 6.9 |
|  | wage rates | + 6.4 | + 8.8 | + 5.5 |
| Prices: | Home | + 5.2 | + 8.5 | + 7.2 |
|  | Export | + 7.5 | + 10.2 | + 9.0 |

This is not always easy. Suppose a UK tile manufacturer is considering the environment in which he is likely to be working. He is not only concerned with real disposable income and other features of the UK economy, but also with the state of the Italian building industry because the largest share of West European tile production originates in Italy. What happens in that domestic market is vital. It probably means that the manager of this business willl have to ask his forecaster to advise him specially on these issues, as they are not a normal feature of published figures.

## Scenarios

In order to work out the effect of different futures, the planner starts with a business plan based on the base-case. He then changes the base-case assumptions in a way that he expects will have a significant effect. He then tests out the impact of these alternatives on the plan figures. It would, however, be laborious to go through the whole planning exercise right down to the sales and production forecasts for each new assumption, and from a practical point of view managers would mutiny at such a prospect. So short cuts have to be found. The relationship between the business and its environment has to be simulated by models.

These models may be as crude or as sophisticated as the complexity of the situation and style of management demands. They could be written on the back of an envelope, such as a 1:1 relationship between manufacturing output in the economy generally and demand for a specific product; or they could be produced by a computer and represent a mathematical equation of considerable complexity.[9] What is important is to get a handle on the critical elements.

For example, one of Conglom's divisions manufactures trucks in the UK. The market influences are complex. These include:

• The cost of steel: this is an energy intensive product.

- Wage rate inflation: UK vehicle manufacturing in the past has been a sector of low productivity as a result of strong demarcations, militant unionization and weak management; in consequence, it has been difficult to abate the effect of wage increases through productivity improvement. Profits were more at the mercy of external fluctuations because wage costs did not flex in response to the level of economic activity—employment costs were a fixed and rising element of the total.
- The impact of rising fuel costs on the demand for motor vehicles (and particularly of vehicles of different engine capacities and operating efficiencies): fuel economy is a major selling point in modern vehicles. During the major oil crises, there was an impact upon total demand within the economy because of the reduction in the amount of spending power, but the vehicles sector was one which was also directly affected by fuel prices.

A simulation based on this has been constructed for the demand side of UK light vehicles.[10] This assumes that the main influences upon demand are real disposable incomes and the real price of fuel. By using this model, Conglom can try out different levels for these factors—a 20 per cent uplift in fuel prices, a major income tax cut or anything else that will impact upon them. In a properly constructed model of the total business, the resultant changes in such variables as price index for motor vehicles, wage rates within the economy, raw material (steel) prices will be determined. A reasonably consistent and complete picture of market conditions within which the business is to operate can be prepared. It is possible then for Conglom to conclude how these factors will influence the profitability of its own business and act accordingly. The simulation mentioned does not go as far as this. The way in which it was used in 1980, to look at some of the external forces that were critical at that time is discussed later in this chapter.

## Cyclicality

Another feature of the macroeconomic scene which is important in the understanding of the market (and the construction of any adequate model) is the way in which economic activity moves around an underlying trend.

Figure 8.3 traces the history of two major national indices since 1972, based on fiscal years. The graph demonstrates how inflation has cycled up and down over the period. The peak occurred in 1975, before dropping to a trough in 1978, then up again in 1980, before reducing to the present level.

The other side of this particular coin is growth, and the graph in Fig. 8.4 shows the way in which the national economy has grown over the same period. Note how 1974/1975 and 1980/1981 each saw a drop in growth, and this coincided with the peaks of the inflationary cycle. Nonetheless, the overall picture is of a continuing underlying growth, albeit at a very slow pace.

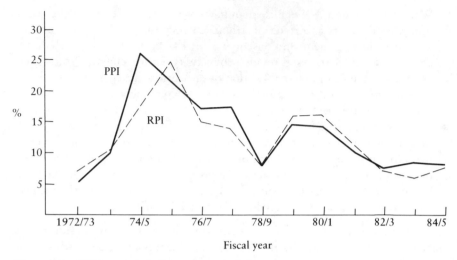

**Figure 8.3**    UK economic indices: percentage change per annum

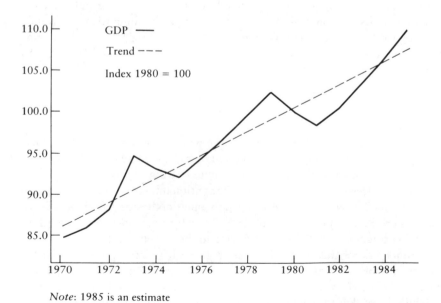

*Note*: 1985 is an estimate

**Figure 8.4**    UK GDP at constant factor cost 1980 prices (average estimate)

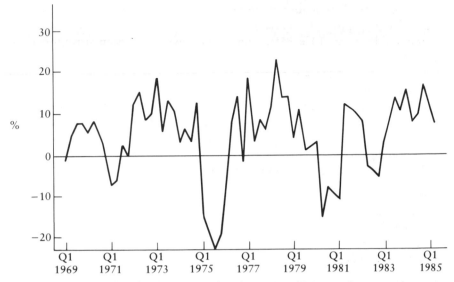

**Figure 8.5**    UK market for printing and writing papers. Quarterly percentage rate change

## The trade cycle

This movement up and down about the underlying trend, called the trade cycle, was described in Chapter 2. The period of the full cycle is between four and five years. All the component businesses within the economy, whether they be trucks or plastic pipe manufacture tend to cycle over the same period, but not necessarily in unison. There is no certainty or precision about the timing in individual sectors or (as a result) in the economy as a whole. This is a great problem for forecasters. Often their predictions come to pass, but later or earlier than they had predicted. Another difficulty they face is the assessment of how strong the recovery will be, or how deep the depression. Yet another area of uncertainty is the direction of the underlying trend. All these movements are difficult to ascertain in periods of turbulence.

Another feature contributing to confusion is seasonality. Peaks of commercial activity occur during the spring and autumn in many businesses. For decorating products, March/April are the key months, for children's books, summer for the publishers and late autumn for the bookstores, but each also tends to have an uplift in the spring season, as well. If seasonality is added to the trade cycles, it is a very wavy line that describes activity in the market (see Fig. 8.5).

## Analysing a market

At the individual sector level, there are, in addition to these overall movements, a mass of individual actions made by management to increase or reduce demand for their products. These may be competitive schemes such as bingo, introduced by most of Fleet Street into their newspapers as an attempt both to gain market share and to halt the overall decline in revenue from circulation sales, or concerted market promotions, such as those undertaken by English cheese and fruit producers.

In all markets there are, furthermore, the random events, unplanned, many undesirable, such as a major strike or a fire at a depot, creating temporary shortages of materials in the industry. These events obscure attempts to analyse what is going on.

Thus, summarizing all the above, the following factors are relevant:

- underlying trend
- trade cycle
- seasonality
- market actions
- random events

The only evidence for the future performance of the economy as a whole, or any component market sector, is what has happened in the past. The task of analysts is to disentangle all these forces and to try to make clear what are the critical elements.

Statistical method, adopting trial and error procedures (based none the less on some rational explanation) enables the skilled researcher to get very close to predicting the behaviour of a market. As an example, a model of the consumer magazines market is shown in Fig. 8.6.[11]

Taking a part of this, Fig. 8.7 depicts the graph of advertising demand in this same consumer magazines market showing the actual level of demand in the solid line, and that predicted by the model in the broken line. It is a close fit which indicates that the analyst has captured the most important influences and that some considerable reliance may be placed on the predictions, provided that the main underlying economic assumptions are correct.

### Scenarios for Conglom

The use of scenarios to explore the effects of change on the truck division of Conglom can now be developed further. Table 8.2 sets out the important details of this business (the data were prepared in 1979, but still serve as a useful illustration).

It is evident that the planner for this business, projecting a rapidly increasing profit margin, has failed to grasp that 1980 was likely to see a normal cyclical downturn in the level of activity in the market place. Leaving this aside, however, Conglom was more concerned about the possibility of another major oil price rise in the first year of the plan. As a result, it tried out the effect of a 30

SALES                                        ADVERTISING

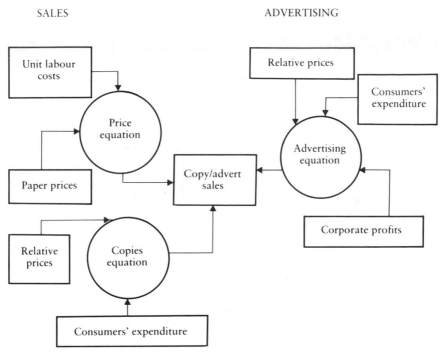

**Figure 8.6**   A consumer magazine model

per cent increase which in the event proved to be a gross understatement! None the less the resultant changes in GDP growth in the economy and in the WPI were indicative of the sort of impact that could be expected. This oil price rise scenario was developed for a full alternative set of assumptions, but the figures in Table 8.3 give a feel for the magnitude of change. In the last year, no altern- ative assumptions are made and the 1980 price rise is seen to have worked its way through the economy so that growth is beginning to move back to the pre- viously forecast rate and inflation has abated to the originally projected rate. This scenario is described further in Chapter 15.

The impact on Conglom's truck division forecast of the changes was esti- mated as seen in Table 8.4. Thus sales dip substantially. Compared with plan indices of 100, 97 and 94 for the three plan years, sales volumes were 87, 83 and 89 respectively, as the adverse environment bites in years 1 and 2 and then starts to ameliorate. This, combined with a lag in cutting back on working capital, results in a much worse cash flow—cumulatively £(1.8)m compared with plan £4.1m. This is a massive swing of almost £6m. Fixed assets do not change as increased expenditure resulting from higher prices is offset by increased de- preciation, taken account of in the activity profit figures. Altogether, this repre- sents a devasting picture for this business.

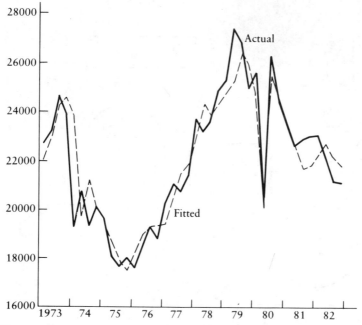

**Figure 8.7**    Consumer magazines real advertising revenues (1973 £'000s)

**Table 8.2**    Summary of performance

| £m | Actual | Plan | | |
|---|---|---|---|---|
| | 1979 | 1980 | 1981 | 1982 |
| Sales | 26.6 | 28.4 | 30.3 | 31.1 |
| Depreciation | 0.3 | 0.4 | 0.4 | 0.5 |
| Employment costs | 7.8 | 8.3 | 8.6 | 9.2 |
| Energy costs | 2.9 | 3.2 | 3.7 | 4.1 |
| Raw material costs | 10.4 | 11.0 | 11.8 | 12.3 |
| Trading profit | 0.6 | 1.2 | 1.4 | 1.8 |
| Average working capital | 8.8 | 7.9 | 8.2 | 8.4 |
| Capital expenditure | 0.6 | 0.4 | 0.5 | 0.8 |
| Fixed assets | 6.0 | 6.0 | 6.1 | 6.4 |
| Trading cash flow | 0.2 | 1.9 | 1.0 | 1.2 |

Table 8.3    Alternative assumptions

| % changes per annum | Base-case | | Oil crisis | |
|---|---|---|---|---|
| | GDP | WPI | GDP | WPI |
| 1980 | −0.5 | 10.3 | −3.4 | 12.5 |
| 1981 | 1.9 | 10.3 | −2.8 | 15.0 |
| 1982 | 4.0 | 9.4 | 3.0 | 9.4 |

Table 8.4    Summary of performance under scenario

| £m | Actual | Scenario | | |
|---|---|---|---|---|
| | 1979 | 1980 | 1981 | 1982 |
| Sales | 26.6 | 24.7 | 23.5 | 25.2 |
| Trading profit | 0.6 | 0.3 | (1.3) | (0.4) |
| Average working capital | 8.8 | 8.2 | 7.8 | 8.2 |
| Fixed assets | 6.0 | 6.0 | 6.1 | 6.4 |
| Trading cash flow | 0.2 | 0.7 | (1.3) | (1.2) |

## Response to scenarios

The point of such exploration is not just to know within reasonable probability what may happen to this business, but to enable its managers and the managers of Conglom itself to think through appropriate reactions to such events. The plan represents the expected environment; the scenarios are alternative futures. The degree to which alternative actions are prepared is dependent on the likelihood that some triggering event will occur and that if it does, it will have a significant effect. It may not be necessary to formalize action to any extent. It may be sufficient to think through the possibilities and to be aware of what options are available.

What are the options? As a general judgement, strategies will not change as a result of short-term cyclical changes in market demand. They are more influenced by the underlying direction of the markets in which a business operates and should only be modified periodically. There could conceivably be some major event which makes a difference immediately, but the introduction of an invention, long-term changes in price structures and even such matters as the intentions of government to legislate to ban smoking advertising are all examples of events which can be perceived well in advance and avoid the need to take precipitate action.

Of more immediate impact, as the economy moves into recession, are the following tactical actions designed to protect cash flow. The order suggests a rough priority.

- postpone capital expenditure/acquisitions;
- cut inventories;
- prolong payables;
- borrow;
- take down-time;
- lay off staff;
- extend credit (to ensure the customers survive);
- dispose of/close plant;
- cut dividends.

Thus Conglom may undertake any of these actions to see its truck business through a recession, but for the long term, it may decide that the UK truck market is not worth the effort and dispose of the business while it still has some value.

## Conclusion

The last two decades have left their mark on most forecasters. As a result, the preoccupation is with the problems thrust up by a hostile rather than by a friendly environment. It is, nevertheless, feasible to adopt the same approach to major beneficial changes in the economic scene. Such a situation, however, is less urgent and is one that most managers would be happy to leave on one side until they see it likely to happen!

This discussion of the environment is necessarily limited by space. The emphasis has been on economic influences. Technological, social and political changes can all be treated in the same way, provided that the events described can be translated into supply and demand terms for the business as well as strictly financial terms such as interest and exchange rates. The endeavour is to:

- simplify the planning process by focusing on critical issues;
- enable the response to events outside the control of the business to be planned in advance.

Though no business can hope to eliminate surprise, a lot can be done in this way to reduce it and thereby give competitive advantage over those who have not thought things through.

## Notes

1. *The Economist*, January 1973, London.
2. Bannock, Baxter and Rees, *Dictionary of Economics*, Penguin, Harmondsworth, 1972, p. 215.
3. The RPI components are defined in the *Employment Guide*, Department of Employment, London, October 1975.

4. These data are available through data banks such as Data Resources Inc./Europe Database and are compiled from a number of official sources.

5. *Report of the Inflation Accounting Committee* (The Sandilands Report) Cmnd 6225, HMSO, London, 5 September 1975.

6. For a discussion of CCA accounting, see D. A. Mallinson, *Understanding CCA Accounting*, Butterworth, London, 1980.

7. W. J. Chandler and P. H. W. Cockle, *Techniques of Scenario Planning*, McGraw-Hill, Maidenhead, Berks, 1982.

8. For example, Data Resources Inc. for international models and London Business School, Cambridge Econometrics or Henley Centre for Forecasting for the UK.

9. *Techniques of Scenario Planning*, op. cit.

10. Constructed by Economic Models Ltd. (now part of Data Resources Inc.). See *Techniques of Scenario Planning*, op. cit. at p. 115.

11. P. H. W. Cockle, *Consumer Magazine Model*, a private paper for Reed International PLC, July 1984.

# 9

# Restructuring the portfolio

Almost all businesses, apart from very small ones like the east-end whelk stall, are involved in more than one market sector. The local garage services commercial as well as private vehicles and sells spares in competition with the high street specialist; the electricity showroom deals in consumer appliances in competition with the department stores, as well as servicing the sale of electricity. To some extent, therefore, all commercial organizations, in addition to growing or reducing their presence in their existing market places, have some options to increase or reduce the number of market sectors they serve, though some adopt a more restricted policy than others. A garage may expand into fast foods and confectionery, electricity showrooms into microprocessors and energy control systems. This chapter is concerned with the mechanics of planning to change the portfolio of markets served—whether by adding to it by acquisition or by internal development; by reinforcement of any of its existing parts; or by reducing it by disposal.

## The cash flow constraint

The structure of the cash flow system is the first area that needs to be explored in this context. Sales growth, whether by purchasing a business or by developing it from its existing base is constrained by the cash available. Apart from sale of assets or increasing borrowings or share capital, the source of funds for development is the surplus thrown up by trading. As a first step in assessing what this will be, the ROTC for the business averaged over all its activities is a measure of what profit can be extracted from the assets involved. The rates of interest and of tax payable and of the distribution to shareholders may then be applied to this profit level to calculate the cash availability. The logic is demonstrated in Fig. 9.1.

The achievable level of ROTC for any business is related not only to its basic characteristics such as market position and capital intensity, but also to what the rate of inflation may be. Consider the graph in Fig. 9.2. It is assumed that:

- interest averages at 12 per cent;
- the borrowing level (debt–equity ratio) is 40 per cent and the management does not want to increase it;

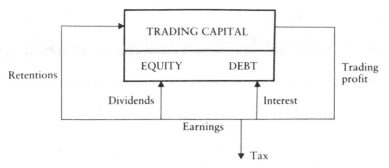

Figure 9.1    The cash flow pipeline

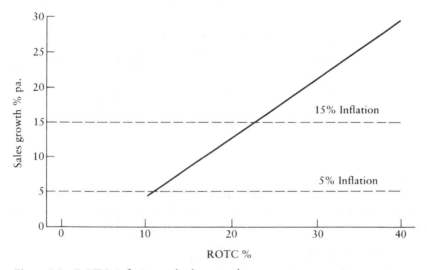

Figure 9.2    ROTC, inflation and sales growth

- the effective tax rate is 35 per cent of profit before tax;
- the dividend paid is 15 per cent of profit before tax.

On this basis, the diagonal line indicates the relationship between ROTC and the sales growth that the company can support. The broken lines in the graph indicate two different levels of inflation. Average rates have been adopted in each case for the sake of simplicity. If the returns are below the broken lines, they will be inadequate in the inflationary regimes indicated to enable the business to keep pace with inflation, that is to provide the additional cash needed to replace fixed and working capital. Real growth can only start if returns lie above the broken line.

What is evident is that the ROTC needed to sustain real growth moves sharply upwards as inflation rises. At inflation of 15 per cent and above, as occurred in the 'seventies, internally funded real growth becomes difficult because of the high returns needed to generate enough cash. In such a situation, assets or businesses may have to be sold, or borrowing limits may have to be raised to sustain even inflationary, let alone real, growth. At present levels of inflation of around 5 per cent, however, the ROTC needed to generate real growth on the basis given above is significantly lower.

Any business can prepare a similar diagram based on its own key assumptions, to show what growth is feasible given its expected ROTC and it can vary some of the assumptions to see what would be the effect—for example, reducing the distribution of profit, releasing the borrowing constraint or selling something off. Individual projects have then to be set into this context, to ensure that the business can actually support the whole set of activities in which it is (or expects to be) invested.

There are some very sophisticated programmes for the analysis of a portfolio (see Chapter 13), but a simple review on the above basis, coupled with a good grasp of the realistic profitability of each business in the portfolio will give a sufficient feel for the overall potential. However, even if this more pragmatic way of assessing the total business is adopted, a structured approach, including specific criteria, is needed for the review of projects for acquisition, internal growth, or disposals.

## Growth by acquisition

Suppose that management has decided that it wishes to enlarge its market presence by acquisition, what are the criteria that it should apply to its search? These may be grouped into three areaa:

- operating performance;
- financial impact;
- cultural fit.

### OPERATING PERFORMANCE

An important feature of setting performance standards lies in the long-term contribution an acquisition is going to make to the business. ROTC is again a primary measure in that it encompasses the effect of both the profit and loss account and the balance sheet in one ratio. Very broadly it can be used as a marker of the trading health of the business, but a further merit from the point of view of a potential acquirer is that it is easy to ascertain from published accounts. The use of other ratios is discussed in Chapter 16.

A business that has a low ROTC, bought for recovery and that does respond to treatment is probably the quickest way of improving overall returns and a bargain price may be the key to success. If, however, that business has no prospect for significant improvement, it is a bad buy, even if it can be purchased at a substantial discount on balance sheet value: it will be unable to provide enough cash long term for its own maintenance, let alone to make any contribution to corporate interest, tax and dividends. The fact that the assets may be purchased at such substantial discount is a delusion; assets have only a value to the extent they can generate profit, though this may be in some other business area than that in which they are currently used, as is the case of property.

If the company is seeking to expand through acquisition, the sales growth of the takeover candidate is an essential performance criterion. Getting bigger by acquisition is not in itself going to provide earnings growth: on a good purchase, earnings may dip initially. It is only when the new business starts to generate the opportunity to make high returns upon its own increasing sales that the desired benefit will come about. The best buys are those that give a continuing opportunity to invest at a high rate of return. It is necessary, therefore, to look for the potential for real sales increases (i.e. sales volumes/mix improvements).

Figure 9.3 illustrates how two investments perform, both with an ROS of 10 per cent, but Company A with 2 per cent pa. sales growth and an ROTC of 25 per cent; and Company B, 10 per cent pa. growth and an ROTC of 22 per cent. Year 0 is the year of purchase and both have a similar profit in that year. Though the faster developing business may have had a lower four-year average profit record up to that date, it is clear that it is much more valuable to a prospective purchaser.

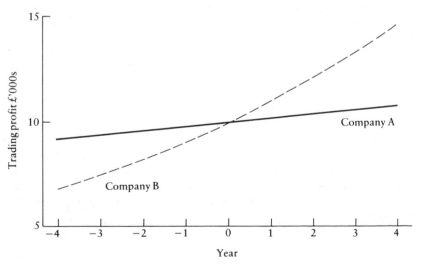

**Figure 9.3**  Profit opportunity

FINANCIAL IMPACT

Conglom would have little difficulty in finding enough money to acquire Plinmo, but a takeover of Conglom by Plinmo is virtually impossible. There are instances of reverse takeovers, where the large company buys the smaller and the management of the latter then asumes control. Such instances are very rare, however, and their contemplation may be left to the compilers of modern corporate myths.

The price to be paid is itself a consequence of the history of growth and returns which the candidate has exhibited. Despite Conglom's capacity to acquire Plinmo, there are a number of other questions that have to be asked in deciding whether it may be desirable to do so. These are:

• How will the price paid affect the balance sheet?
• Will the gearing ratio be affected?
• Will earnings per share be diluted?

The question of price raises the issue of price–earnings ratios (PER). Where a share is quoted on the Stock Exchange, the price that is currently being paid for the shares is shown as a ratio of the earnings. The extract in Table 9.1 is taken from the *Financial Times* of 4 January 1985.

Table 9.1    London share prices, FT 4 January 1984

| 1984–85 | | | | + or | Div | | Y'ld | |
| High | Low | Stock | Price | − | Net | C'vr | Gr's | P/E |
|---|---|---|---|---|---|---|---|---|
| 261 | 202 | Vaux | 258xd | −4 | 10.06 | 2.2 | 5.6 | 10.1 |
| 217 | 128 | Whitbread 'A' | 211 | −4 | 6.25 | 2.6 | 4.2 | 10.6 |
| 272 | 206 | Wolv. & Dudley | 270xd | | 7.6 | 3.0 | 4.0 | 11.7 |
| 280 | 220 | Young Brew 'A' 50p | 240 | | 5.5 | 2.0 | 3.3 | 21.4 |
| 180 | 120 | Do. Non. V. 50p | 165 | | 5,.5 | 2.0 | 4.8 | 14.7 |

In this instance, Young Breweries has a much higher rating than the others. This indicates that it is more highly valued by the investing public. This may be for a variety of reasons, e.g. an incipient bid, an expectation of a high dividend pay-out, a sudden dip in profit on which the PER is based which is seen as one-off; or it may be an expectation for continuing rapid earnings growth. From such data it is possible to start the process of assessing a realistic offer price for a company, bearing in mind that a premium will have to be paid over the market capitalization.

What this premium is likely to be is also affected by the state of the market at the time of the offer. Thus:

• a buoyant stock market

- a highly rated business
- competition from other bidders
- opposition from the candidate

are all factors which can take the price premium soaring. So in December 1985 the *Investors Chronicle* commented that Wedgwood, the fine china manufacturer, should reach a share price of 228p (a PER of 8). The following April the shares had risen to 368p (PER 13) following a hostile bid by London International valued at 328p. They sagged to 325p after referral of the bid to the Monopolies Commission and rose again to 371p when Pentland announced that it would act as a 'white knight' to help fend off the unwelcome suitor. All the factors mentioned save an initial high rating, were present, and London International had the added interest that it already owned Royal Worcester china manufacturers.

A high PER may be justified in such a situation if the business can be linked as in this example with another to improve market position or where growth and returns are dramatically high. But even with good growth and a high ROTC it would take several years to achieve an acceptable return on investment. It may make life an immediately richer experience to own such a company, but the shareholders of the acquiring company will have a long wait to be richer in dividends as a result.

Where a business is not quoted, the assessment of price may be more difficult. In any bid, the floor price will be what the business is worth to the seller and the ceiling is what it is worth to the buyer. In between is the negotiating ground. There is a tendency on the part of many bidders to consider only what is the maximum they are willing to pay. In a recent transaction by Swedish Match, the management approached the price question in a scientific way. They undertook a careful analysis of the value of the business to the sellers and in so doing, saved themselves several million dollars on the price they were prepared to pay.[1]

At the bottom of the performance scale, a company being bought for recovery may have been making losses and a PER is not possible, though it might be worked out on a prospective basis. In such a case, an assessment is normally made of the asset value. Stocks and debtors will have some value if the business can be continued as a going concern. The value of plant and equipment is more problematic. In business, the only value that fixed assets have is their profit generating capacity, though, as indicated, they may have an alternative use value. There has to be an estimated future profit potential from them. This may be judged from experience. There are, however, techniques for assessing profit potential of the undertaking and these are discussed in Chapter 13. One such technique measures the characteristics of the business to be acquired along such dimensions as market position and capital intensity, and matches the results with those of other businesses in the Strategic Planning Institute's LIM model.[2]

A view may be gained thereby on what profit may be expected and this will give clues as to the potential of the business. If the sort of PER appropriate to the sector in which the activity is operating is then ascertained, the ceiling price may be established.

*Testing the impact*

Once the price bracket is decided, the financial impact on the acquiring company can be assessed. There are three matters to examine:

- the effect on the trading results of the parent group of a straightforward consolidation of the acquired company;
- the balance sheet effect of the difference between the purchase price and the net asset value of the new business (goodwill or cost of control);
- the differing effects of settling the purchase price in shares of the parent company or in cash.

Suppose that Conglom wished to make a takeover bid for Plinmo. The outline of the transaction might be as set out in Table 9.2, based on the Year 5 figures for both companies as shown in the accounts in Appendix 1.

**Table 9.2**    Acquisition analysis, Plinmo Limited

| | |
|---|---|
| • Price | PER of 10, giving £2.2m |
| • Cost of control | £0.2m; the purchase price splits 58% fixed assets, 32% working capital, 10% cost of control |
| • Price payable all in cash, borrowed at 12% interest. | |

Consolidation would give the key figures in Table 9.3. Note 3 has a very marked effect on the debt–equity ratio. In Conglom's case, it increases from 75 per cent to 99 per cent. This raises an already high gearing excessively and unless it can be seen from a convincing review of the potential of the business that it will rapidly reduce, the deal must be ruled out on a cash basis. Conglom would have to consider whether it could undertake a takeover using shares. On the same assumptions as above, but, additionally, taking Conglom to have 6 million shares in issue which have a low PER rating of 7 (because of poor past performance), the different effect on the consolidated figures would be as shown in Table 9.4. Conglom improves its debt–equity ratio, but the last line in the table indicates the level of dilution of the shareholders' interest that would occur. This is just about tolerable and is something which shareholders could accept, provided there was a very real probability of improvement from the deal in a short space of time.

Table 9.3    Impact of acquisition, Plinmo Limited

| £m | Conglom | Plinmo | Adjustments | Consolidated |
|---|---|---|---|---|
| Sales | 66.8 | 2.6 | | 69.4 |
| Trading profit | 5.2 | 0.3 | | 5.5 |
| Trading cash flow | 2.7 | 0.1 | | 2.8 |
| Earnings | 2.5 | 0.2 | (0.1) | 2.6 |
| Working capital | 13.5 | 0.7 | | 14.2 |
| Fixed assets | 15.0 | 1.3 | | 16.3 |
| Cost of control | 4.1 | | 0.2 | 4.3 |
| Debt | 12.3 | 0.6 | 2.2 | 15.1 |
| Equity | 16.3 | 1.3 | (2.4) | 15.2 |
| D–E ratio % | 75 | 46 | | 99 |

*Notes*
1  Consolidated earnings are reduced by the interest (less tax on the amount of the purchase price.
2  Equity is reduced for calculating D–E ratio by the amount of the cost of control.
3  On a cash purchase, debt is increased and equity is reduced by the amount of the purchase price.

Table 9.4    Impact of acquisition, Plinmo (amended)

| £m | Conglom | Plinmo | Adjustments | Consolidated |
|---|---|---|---|---|
| Earnings | 2.5 | 0.2 | | 2.7 |
| Debt | 12.3 | 0.6 | | 12.9 |
| Equity | 16.3 | | 2.0 | 18.3 |
| D–E ratio % | 75 | 46 | | 70 |
| Shares issued '000s | 6000 | | 754 | 6754 |
| Earnings per share p | 41.7 | | | 38.5 |

On the basis shown, it looks as though Conglom would manage through such a move to get quite a benefit. The questions not only of price and relative values, but also of how the deal is to be implemented are critical for their effect on the key ratios of the consolidated business.

CULTURAL FIT
Cultural fit is the third area for considering the appropriateness of any acquisition. This phrase covers all the wide variety of non-quantifiable factors which are, nonetheless, critical to the decision, to buy or not to buy. The sort of questions to address are:

• Can the existing strategies of the business acquired continue without major revision? If the objective is a recovery, then it may be essential to be able to change them; if it is to diversify into a new sector in which the parent management does not have much experience, it is essential that they continue unchanged—there is little point in buying a successful business in order to pull it to pieces.

- Is the existing management satisfactory? The same sort of considerations apply here as in the previous question. If the managers are needed, will they stay? A large organization like Conglom might have difficulty in persuading a successful Jack Robinson to carry on working if they have made him rich as a result of the takeover.
- Is the sort of business acquired something that the rest of the organization can live with? A publisher of women's magazines a number of years ago, faced with the opportunity to develop into the profitable market of soft porn, turned it down after a half-hearted experiment, because it was quite contrary to the image and attitudes of the group.
- Is the new activity something with which the parent company management team feels comfortable? Many planners have beaten their brains out on the brick wall of chief executive obstinacy. What appears to them to be a good opportunity slips through the corporate grasp because the top person will not do it. In the end, the decision has to be that of the chief executive and if he or she feels intuitively that there is something about the deal that is wrong, that is an end to it.

Thus, in seeking to implement any strategy to grow by acquisition, there is a wide variety of filters through which any specific proposal must pass successfully before it can be accepted as a suitable business to buy.

## Capital expenditure

The discussion turns now to development projects, by which is meant those grafted onto the existing business, rather than maintenance projects devoted only to keeping the existing business going. The focus is on proposals to change the balance of the markets served. Any development proposal should be generated out of the planning process, rather than superimposed upon it. The frequent introduction of unplanned projects is a sign of inadequate management; the strategies that justify the project should have already been set. Provided the project conforms to these, there will be no need to be concerned with any criteria other than trading and financial performance.

The trading performance issues have already been raised in the context of market tactics and acquisition performance. On the financial side, the most frequently applied criterion for capital projects is that of internal rate of return (IRR). This is based on the evaluation of the cash flow over a number of years and on calculation of the rate of return of the cash income as compared to the cash outgo.[3] The IRR is that discount rate, as a percentage and calculated over a chosen number of years, that brings the net cost of trading capital and all income into equality. An alternative way of looking at this is to calculate the net present value of the project which shows the present value of income, less out-go, discounted at the chosen rate.

There are two questions for planners:

- which cash flow stream to analyse;
- what level to set for minimum acceptable IRR.

The choice of cash flow streams lies between the total and the incremental. The total cash flow approach incorporates the project in the whole forward projection of the business and does not seek to identify the extra cash flow realized from the additional cash investment made. The incremental approach seeks to make such identification .

Suppose the manager of Plinmo's motor accessories business wanted to increase the capacity of his production line. Ignoring for the moment that the agreed strategy is to reduce this activity, it could quite readily be shown that a new machine, sharing common services and using the existing labour force could operate at a good incremental return on the additional capital employed—provided the additional product could be sold. Even so, the total return on the business is likely to remain inadequate. The utility of investing further in an unattractive business has to be addressed by looking at the totality.

On the other side of the coin are the highly successful businesses where an incremental project may not be able to achieve anywhere near as good a return as the existing operations. This may be the case in business publishing, because of the low capital intensity. The proposal to computerize part of the business sector data base may look completely unacceptable on a stand-alone basis, while if mingled with the overall figures, the effect is likely to be lost and over-looked. In such a situation, the incremental returns must be separately assessed. The project may prove to be the right thing to do to protect the long-term future of the business, but it should only be done after an individual analysis. Whether it is desirable to concentrate on total or incremental cash flows is, therefore, a question to be decided in each particular case. In any event, both sets of calculations should be prepared.

On the second question, the financial performance, the minimum rate of return should be whatever can be achieved by an alternative use of the money, at no greater risk. If there is surplus cash available in the company, this will be the rate receivable on gilt-edged or similar securities. In fact, since this is theoretically a no-risk investment, funds put into anything which does not offer a guaranteed return should be required to give a better return, according to assessment of risk. There is no formula for calculating this; it is a matter for personal judgement.

If, however, the sponsors of a number of projects are competing among themselves for limited funds, then the project to support is obviously that which offers the best rate of return above the threshold rate described, again allowing for risk. If Plinmo proposes to get into the market for car bumpers, the returns offered may be high, but the state of the UK motor industry may be such as to require a substantial discount to be applied to the returns in comparison with other projects, to take account of the uncertainties.

The period over which the calculations are to be made is another important qualification. It is not normally worth considering any cash flow beyond 10 years, as the impact at such a remote time on the IRR will be minimal. There will be special cases that are back-end loaded, where income only begins to flow after, say, seven years and builds up quickly to massive proportions. On the other hand, it is inadequate to take less than five years for any assessment and it is probably worth running the figures out for the full ten in all cases.

An advantage of this is that on conclusion of the investment, any resale value of the asset is normally taken into account. At a 10-year horizon, this 'guesstimate' will have less of an impact on the figures than if it were taken at an earlier date. In view of the speculative nature of the valuation, this is a more desirable approach. Where the asset will only last for a shorter time-scale, that briefer period will have to be adopted if it is a one-off project. Otherwise, it would be necessary to provide for the replacement as part of the cash flow of the project.

Finally, even if the project beats all the rest proposed by the businesses in the company's portfolio, it still has to reach a level of return that will contribute to the general objectives of the business as discussed above. The required IRR to equate to the ROTC goal derived from the graph in Fig. 9.2 is not readily calculated directly from that ROTC. It is easier to go back to the same basic data and work out separately the IRR which corresponds to an acceptable average ROTC.

The important thing to bear in mind, however, when doing all these calculations—indeed any calculations—is that the criteria that they provide are only general guidelines. They add to knowledge and understanding of a project, but there are still cases where some special circumstance, such as pre-empting a competitor, will mean the acceptance or rejection of a proposal, notwithstanding the numbers.

## Assessing disposals

There are three technical factors to look at in undertaking strategies for disposal of businesses:

- setting the price;
- timing;
- the impact on the total business.

All of the three are very closely intertwined.

The minimum price is again dependent on the evaluation of alternative cash flow streams—with and without the business. The minimum price receivable will then be the figure that equates the 'sell' with the 'retain' stream. For example, Conglom wishes to sell its truck division. The planned cash flow over the next three years is a total of £4.1m. Discounted at the going financing rate, this has a present value of, say, £3.6m. (Three years is rather a short time-scale, but serves to indicate the method.) The disposal, furthermore, will release some property which may be sold for £0.3m. Assuming no other income or outgo, the minimum price would be the sum of £3.6m and £0.3m, i.e. £3.9m. In view of the oil price scenario and other doubts about the plans of the business, this may be optimistic. On the other hand, there is £8m or so working capital, some of which must be recoverable. So perhaps £4m may be the right figure.

Returning to the general theme, the floor price is not necessarily the price at which to sell; as indicated above, this must also be dependent on the value to the purchaser. The floor price only represents the level below which it is better to retain the business. The ceiling price in such situation could be higher and it is essential to examine the potential of the business to the prospective purchaser to try to work out how much this could be. Had the sellers to Swedish Match in the case cited earlier, thought this through, they could have obtained a much better price.

There may also be another constraint upon the sale value, and that is the impact of write-off on the debt–equity ratio of the company as a whole. While it ought to be recognized that once the value of a business has been diminished through low profitability, it should properly be written off at once, this is an austere philosophy which few observe to the letter. Indeed, in the truck division case given above, a sale at the floor price would mean a write-off for Conglom of about £12.5m. This could not be absorbed when its total equity is only £16.3m. Consequently, if sale for a low price means a big write-off, there is a strong incentive to postpone disposal until a more favourable time, or indeed perpetually. It is this problem which has a compelling influence upon the timing of such action.

Of tactical importance, also, is the timing to take advantage of best market conditions. If sales or margins are highly cyclical, it is obviously better to show a history starting from the trough and working to the peak of the cycle. The best three years of growth can be shown in this way. Businesses should be sold just as they are beginning to move off the top of the cycle. Furthermore, at this point, most other companies in the sector will have been enjoying a similar buoyancy. Cash becomes less scarce as the boom flattens off and the pay-off on increased working capital is coming through. Buyers are more likely to be flush with confidence and cash at this time.

The overall figures will also be modified by the way in which the earnings respond to the disposal. Normally, when a disposal is undertaken, it is not immediately followed by a re-investment of funds. As a result, the immediate effect will be the difference between what the disposal was contributing and the going interest rate. The cash realized only translates into interest savings at the current market rate, rather than the higher rate generated by investment in a good activity.

Suppose that Plinmo's motor accessories business is making merely 10 per cent ROTC. If the trading capital were to realize only 50 per cent of overall book value on a sale, and this saves interest at 11 per cent, the result is equivalent to an ROTC of just 5.5 per cent. Until the proceeds can be ploughed back into the business at a return in excess of 20 per cent, the earnings will suffer. It is, of course, true that Plinmo should have written off the excess value of the assets in its books, to enable the realizable value to emerge, but it is difficult to assess such value until it is tested in the market place.

Finally, other combinations of returns and realizations may produce beneficial effects even at the money market interest rate. This is certainly the case if some proceeds can be salvaged out of a loss-maker.


## Trawling for acquisitions

This chapter on the mechanics of restructuring a portfolio concludes with a description of methods for finding suitable acquisition candidates. When management has decided that it is seeking to expand its operations by buying a business, it may have some specific opportunity in mind. It will then analyse the detail of such business and is unlikely to want to search further unless the candidate fails to meet its requirements. In such circumstances, it might miss the best buy, but it is far from certain that by extending its search, the ideal opportunity will be found. Commercial life is about seizing good opportunities, not seeking the optimum.

If, however, management has failed in its favoured venture, or has no clear idea from the start about individual companies to buy, it will have to adopt a literature search, looking through the various directories that give clues about suitable candidates, such as:

- Stock Exchange Year Book;
- Kompass Register;
- *The Times* Top 1000.

Having identified some opportunities which look on the face of it to be of interest, these may be examined in more detail from:

- annual report and accounts—for non-quoted companies these are available at the Companies' Registry;
- Moodies and Extel cards;
- data base services on stock exchange information such as Datastream or Compustat.

The first of these three sources covers all companies registered in the UK, but unfortunately many are seriously behind with filing their figures and the information may not be sufficiently up-to-date to be useful. The other two sources are up-to-date as a general rule and the last has the merit of offering an automated trawling service so that by specifying such matters as business sector, size of sales and performance criteria, it is possible to get a print-out of everything that is on the data base which meets these criteria. There are, however, drawbacks in that the data bases cover only a limited number of companies. Ultimately they will cover all businesses, but for the time being, the search for small private undertakings by this means may be frustrated.

Given that the staff are successful in getting the information they want, they will compile this into a report. The following is an example of a major search project. The figures are taken from a real case but they and the name are disguised.

### SHORT FORM REPORT ON EXCO CORPORATION
#### (Prepared 14 May 1982)

*Summary for the Board of Predator Inc*

## 1.  Market

1.1  Exco manufactures power supply units, semiconductors and allied industrial equipment. Forecasts for the market are as follows:

- the power supply unit market is growing in excess of 15 per cent pa.;
- semiconductor production is expected to double between 1981 and 1986;
- production of semiconductor wafer-processing equipment is projected to triple in the same period.

1.2  Exco market characteristics are as follows:

- it has a dominant position in the power-supply unit market though that market is fragmented;
- it is technically at least as good as the competition;
- it has a high and unique degree of backward vertical integration.

## 2.  Performance

2.1  Exco's recent track record is excellent:

- For the first four years real sales growth was 17 per cent pa.: the slow-down in 1981 reduced the overall figure to 12 per cent pa.;
- ROTC has averaged 36 per cent and shows good stability.

2.2    The effect of the recession can be seen in the following figures:

|  | 1977 | 1978 | 1979 | 1980 | 1981 |
|---|---|---|---|---|---|
| Index of real sales | 100 | 124 | 149 | 158 | 153 |

2.3    Exco has weathered the recession much better than many other electronics-based companies, and though trading profit dipped slightly in 1981 on sales up 6 per cent, working capital was held constant and ROTC was well over 30 per cent as it has been in every one of the last five years.

2.4    The semiconductor division (with an ROTC of about 17 per cent) has performed slightly less well than the other divisions, but action is being taken—see pp. *xx* of the published accounts.

## 3.   Price

3.1    The PER of around 13 for this business may seem high* but bearing in mind its ROTC and market growth rate this is not excessive; Exco is not a glamour stock.

3.2    Predator would have to buy for all cash: this would add 15 per cent to trading profits and would raise its D–E ratio to around 60 per cent.

3.3    The present share price is $6.66. In 1981 the high was $16 and the low $6.62; in 1980 the high was $14.80 and the low $5.25.

3.4    In the last 12 months the price has fallen by 52 per cent while light electronics shares overall fell by 23 per cent and the New York Index of all companies fell by 13 per cent.

## 4.   Management

4.1    All executive managers are well regarded and are in the age bracket 35–50. The Chairman is 69 and owns 17 per cent of the company.

## 5.   Rationale

5.1    This is a move by Predator into a contiguous market. It provides a significant opportunity for fruitful vertical integration with Sigma Division.

5.2    The management is perceived as capable of continuing its successful strategies for growth and there is no need to strengthen them or make any dramatic change in direction.

*The stock market was significantly lower at this time (May 1982)

**Basic Statistics**

| Accounts Data | Year Ended 28/9/81 |
| --- | --- |
| Turnover | $55.5m |
| Trading profit | $10.6m |
| Trading capital | $32.6m |
| ROTC | 32.3% |
| Capital intensity | 59.0% |
| Fixed capital intensity | 17.9% |
| Debt–equity ratio | 10.0% |

| Company value | |
| --- | --- |
| Market capitalization | $59.0m |
| PER | 12.6 |

| Market data | |
| --- | --- |
| Real sales growth rate | 12% pa. |
| Market growth rate | 16% pa. |

| Consolidated position | |
| --- | --- |
| % Increase in trading profit | 14.7% |
| Debt–equity post acquisition | 64.2% |
| Maximum price premium for D–E | 1.86 |
| Maximum price premium for dilution | 1.33 |

Note:
Maximum premia for D–E ratio and dilution indicate maxima before the policy constraints adopted by Predator would be broken.

| Recent performance | 1977 | 1978 | 1979 | 1980 | 1981 |
|---|---|---|---|---|---|
| Sales $m | 24.0 | 32.2 | 44.0 | 52.6 | 55.5 |
| Index of real sales | 100 | 124 | 149 | 158 | 153 |
| ROTC | 36.1% | 38.5% | 37.9% | 36.0% | 32.3% |

| Business segments | Sales % | Tr profit | Est ROTC |
|---|---|---|---|
| Power supplies | 63% | $8.9m | 44% |
| Semiconductors | 10% | $0.5m | 17% |
| Industrial equipment | 27% | $2.3m | 25% |

| Foreign sales | | | |
|---|---|---|---|
| Europe | 16% | 1.8 | 40% |
| Far East | 13% | 1.2 | 24% |
| Other | 1% | — | 0% |

Key management 1981

| Name | Position | Age | Shares % | Remuneration $'000s |
|---|---|---|---|---|
| Alfred NEWMAN | Chairman/founder | 69 | 16.95% | 85 |
| Raoul PROCTOR | President & Chief Executive | 46 | 0.4% | 677 incl. 492 on stock options |
| Edmund BROWN | Executive VP & Chief Op. Officer | 41 | * | 150 |
| Adam BRUNTON | VP Admin & Chief Financial Officer | 49 | 0.3% | 439 incl. 329 on stock options |
| Richard BAYER | VP operations/ind. equipment | 35 | * | 105 |
| John HAGMAN | VP and General Man., Kappa Div. | 35 | * | 138 |
| Other officers & directors | | | 3.9% | |
| Total shares held by insiders | | | 21.5% | |

*Included in other officers and directors

I recommend this project to the Board and attach detailed reports on:

- strategic rationale and opportunities;
- the markets and competition;
- production facilities;
- management and personnel;
- past and projected performance;
- the prospective price;
- financial impact on Predator Inc.

..........................................................15.5.1982
President and Chief Executive

The detailed reports mentioned above are not included here, but it is clear that what was provided was, in effect, a strategic plan for Exco within Predator. It gave the Board a full and clear picture of expectations for the business in the future. Unhappily, in this particular case, they turned the opportunity down!

## Notes
1. J. D. Nielsen, *The Swedish Match Acquisition of Gillette Disposable Lighters*, Paper presented to the PIMS Conference, London, December 1984.
2. B. T. Gale and D. J. Swire, *The Limited Information Report*, Strategic Planning Institute, Cambridge, Mass., 1977.
3. For a discussion of discounted cash flow and allied techniques, see D. Fanning (ed.), *Handbook of Management Accounting*, Gower Press, Aldershot, Hants, 1983, p. 69 *et seq.*

# 10

# The finance plan

## What the plan contains

If Jack Robinson is a successful entrepreneur, one part of his business affairs that he certainly will have sorted out is his financing—how much money he needs to keep it going and where he is going to get it from. Tight control of cash within the business is a feature of the self-made millionaire's style and ought to be so for all undertakings.

In addition to being concerned with cash, the finance plan also deals with a variety of connected areas. The major topics to be discussed under this heading are:

- the raising of funds
- the control of monetary working capital
- exchange exposure
- tax management
- distribution policy
- the share price

Each of these subjects is a specialization in its own right and needs to be studied as such. The purpose of this chapter is to give a few planning angles on the subjects and how they integrate into the planning process.

## Raising funds

The finance plan flows from both the strategic and the tactical plans. The financing of the business overall, or of any specific project within it, will normally have to be organized well in advance. Money is raised in an independent market place, with the rate of interest fluctuating over time. The longer the time horizon within which requirements are planned, the more likely it is that the most advantageous rates can be secured. Furthermore, it has proved to be impossible at certain critical times to raise money at all, as when the government in the last two decades put the squeeze on bank liquidity. So corporate treasurers must emulate the wise virgins and oil their lamps well in advance!

A major decision in raising funds is whether to go for a share issue or for loans. Assuming the availability of equity capital at a reasonable rate, an advantage of financing by this route lies in its beneficial effect on gearing. Issuing

more shares will reduce the debt–equity ratio. This may be particularly important if the purpose is to fund a long-term project which is unlikely to produce
returns for some time. Interest payments are necessarily front-end loaded, that
is they cost more at the beginning of the project in real terms because inflation
gradually erodes the real cost over time. The early payment of full interest
could be an additional burden which a project of the nature described might
not be able to sustain. It only becomes feasible in such circumstances, if investors are found who are willing to put down 'patient' money. The development
in the 'sixties of the Canadian Churchill Falls hydro-electric scheme by British
Newfoundland Corporation was of this nature. Massive injections of capital
were needed at the start and through the whole construction period. The shareholders provided this without any expectation of profit or dividend until the
power scheme came on-stream.

Fund raising by shares does, nevertheless, have a number of disadvantages:

- It may dilute the potential earnings per share. Shares usually have to be
  issued at a discount to the market price. If the proceeds of the issue will
  generate a lower return in the future than is earned on the existing equity
  capital, this reduces earnings on all shares and dilutes the value received by
  the existing shareholders. Investors must be made fully aware of the implications at the time of the issue, and certainly for any major issue the approval
  of existing shareholders would be required.
- The cost of equity capital is, in the long run, potentially more expensive than
  borrowings. Inflation will erode the cost of interest on a fixed interest loan,
  but dividends will normally increase both in response to inflation and to
  satisfy expectations of dividend increases with improving profits.
- A public offering is a complex and expensive procedure, though somewhat
  less so for the unlisted securities market (USM) which is designed for small
  companies and can admit new ventures under certain circumstances.[1]
- Once shares have been issued outside the small family circle, there is the
  danger of losing control and, in any event, the company has to be run on a
  much more arms-length basis.

Not that lenders will allow owners a completely free hand. They will want to
be reassured that their interest and capital is safe. But provided that they can
see that both are adequately covered by the profits and assets of the business,
they will not fret about whether the full resources of the business are being
fruitfully exploited. It is expected at present for a reasonably good risk that
interest will be covered about six times by trading profit.[2] This sounds quite
high, but it means that the business has adequate retentions after interest, tax
and dividends to continue to replace its assets.

DEBT–EQUITY RATIO
The other measure used to control borrowing levels is the debt–equity ratio.

This has been referred to a number of times before, but basically, it gives a feel for the riskiness of the funding of the business. If the ratio is excessively high, it means that in periods of violent fluctuation of interest rates, the company is vulnerable to major financial market changes. Conglom in Year 5 has a debt–equity ratio of 75 per cent. The sudden imposition by government of a minimum lending rate (MLR) of 12 per cent as occurred out of the blue in January 1985, would have added 1.5 per cent to its interest charges. It wipes off at once more than 1 per cent return on investment which also comes straight out of the cash flow. This increase is mild compared to what happened in the mid 'seventies. Many groups, in the wake of the first oil crisis in 1974, found themselves massively overborrowed. D–E ratios were often over 100 per cent as interest rates soared over 20 percent. At the time of writing, around 35 per cent is deemed the prudent limit for the D–E ratio under normal conditions. Anything over that has to be examined with caution. Heavy borrowing should certainly be avoided to fund the ordinary operations of the business.

Many small, fast-growing businesses, wishing to avoid the problems of high gearing and the front-end loading of interest, yet not being of a size or track record to support a public offering, will seek funds in the venture capital market. This involves professional fund managers overseeing the early development of a new business (or recapitalization and relaunch of an old one under new management) within a portfolio of similar investments. It is a well developed source of funds in the USA and is growing in popularity in the UK.[3] Not only does it mean money for the individual entrepreneur, but also a lot of help and guidance from experts.

### Control of monetary working capital

Managing debtors and creditors (referred to here as monetary working capital) is traditionally a task for the finance department. In every market, the length of credit given is set by custom and practice. Those who sell nuclear power stations will probably be in the game of negotiating long-term credit, because that sort of money is not going to be paid over in 30 days. In other areas, the rule may be cash over the counter. In the majority of manufacturing businesses, periods of up to 90 days are quite common.

Export debtors will normally enjoy a longer period of credit than home sales. If the monetary working capital for these is not disentangled from the domestic requirements, it is not possible to assess the benefits of overseas trading. If an extended credit is allied to the longer inventory pipeline, the higher margins in overseas sales may be a delusion.

Suppose Plinmo sells to its home market at 45 per cent gross margin and to its overseas customers at 48 per cent. Its domestic debtors average 60 days and its exports, 120. Its relative stocks are likewise, 30 and 60 days. In such circumstances, the additional 3 per cent margin is more than offset by the financing charges on the additional working capital. Furthermore, there is an outflow of cash at the gross trading profit level for every additional £1 of export sales gained.

It is a normal feature of any recession that debtors will postpone payment longer than during periods of buoyancy. An examination of previous downturns in a market should give some clues as to the extent of this slow-down and the cash implications can be planned accordingly. Some managers may choose to be ready to attack their debtors with everything they have, to get their outstandings in before the crunch comes. It would be naive to assume that everyone can adopt this attitude. A recession necessarily implies a slow-down in business activity and, in particular, a slowing down in the velocity of money round the market place. Some relaxation in credit terms is inevitable. Forewarning of this situation may be exploited by deciding which customers are to receive favoured treatment—some perforce in order to nurse them through the crisis and ensure that they are still in business at the end. This is not altruism, only common sense.

DEBTOR–CREDITOR BALANCE

The balance between debtors and creditors is a key feature of financing the business. Some sectors, as indicated above, will have virtually no debtors, e.g. retail supermarkets. They use their creditors as an important source of finance and are not called upon to fund their debtors at all. At the other end of the scale, there are corporations who choose to settle their bills quickly, but are not over-fast in their collections—which could be through some characteristic of the market place such as intense competition or the size of unit sales. The extent to which different businesses adopt different policies in this connection may be measured by the relative ratios of debtors and creditors to sales.

Tables 10.1 and 10.2 give some examples taken in January 1984 from the Datastream data base. These are a random selection of leading quoted companies in the UK, but they display some of the more extreme characteristics of the debtor–creditor relationship:[4]

If the ratios are then put together as the balance of debtors less creditors to

**Table 10.1**  Debtors to sales percentage

| Year ending in: | 1978 | 1979 | 1980 | 1981 | 1982 | Average |
|---|---|---|---|---|---|---|
| British Leyland | 12.95 | 14.97 | 15.07 | 11.89 | 13.92 | 13.76 |
| Great Universal Stores | 32.63 | 30.21 | 28.63 | 29.86 | 29.21 | 30.11 |
| General Electric Company | 22.45 | 22.78 | 24.90 | 25.22 | 21.80 | 23.43 |
| Imperial Chemical Indust. | 21.62 | 21.33 | 19.69 | 21.14 | 20.37 | 20.83 |
| Sainsbury | 0.67 | 0.64 | 0.84 | 0.63 | 0.50 | 0.66 |
| Unilever | 13.27 | 13.31 | 12.87 | 13.01 | 12.96 | 13.09 |

**Table 10.2**    Creditors to sales percentage

| Year ending in: | 1978 | 1979 | 1980 | 1981 | 1982 | Average |
|---|---|---|---|---|---|---|
| British Leyland | 24.12 | 27.04 | 32.06 | 29.58 | 27.22 | 28.00 |
| Great Universal Stores | 12.99 | 14.41 | 14.22 | 14.89 | 15.05 | 14.31 |
| General Electric Company | 27.63 | 27.05 | 27.68 | 26.81 | 27.38 | 27.31 |
| Imperial Chemical Indust. | 17.21 | 16.56 | 16.12 | 16.73 | 16.09 | 16.54 |
| Sainsbury | 6.85 | 7.63 | 10.28 | 9.19 | 10.51 | 8.89 |
| Unilever | 12.74 | 12.83 | 12.92 | 13.53 | 13.15 | 13.03 |

**Table 10.3**    Debtors less creditors to sales percentage

| Year ending in: | 1978 | 1979 | 1980 | 1981 | 1982 | Average |
|---|---|---|---|---|---|---|
| British Leyland | − 11.17 | − 12.07 | − 16.99 | − 17.69 | − 13.31 | − 14.25 |
| Great Universal Stores | + 19.64 | + 15.81 | + 14.42 | + 14.97 | + 14.16 | + 15.80 |
| General Electric Company | − 5.18 | − 4.27 | − 2.78 | − 1.59 | − 5.59 | − 3.88 |
| Imperial Chemical Indust. | + 3.53 | + 3.64 | + 4.88 | + 6.77 | + 5.62 | + 4.89 |
| Sainsbury | − 6.19 | − 6.99 | − 9.44 | − 8.56 | − 10.01 | − 8.24 |
| Unilever | + 0.53 | + 0.48 | − 0.05 | − 0.52 | − 0.18 | + 0.05 |

sales (Table 10.3), this can be used as a measure of the extent to which monetary working capital has been used to finance operations.

British Leyland shows a high negative value. This means that the proportion of creditors is that much higher than the proportion of debtors. For every £100m of turnover at that time, the percentage represented an average £14m in cash flow retained by the company (though the benefit only occurs once). The Unilever example is neutral; the cash flow is little affected except by phasing and departures from the norm. In the GUS case, with its large mail order business, there is a high positive value, indicating that debtors are much higher than creditors. For every £100m turnover, cash flow approaching £16m was required to fund working capital.

The average for this ratio for all industrial companies in the UK on the Datastream data base over the period 1978–82 was a negative 1.55 per cent, meaning that most companies used creditors to fund their activities to some degree. This average could be used as a yardstick; better still, a measure specific to the sector in which the company does business could be ascertained. It may then be a useful indicator in financial planning of the amount of additional funds which could be available to be pulled out of the business—or of how much might have to be ploughed back.

If ICI, for instance, with its positive ratio of 4.89 per cent had been able to get back to the overall industrial norm, this would have benefited working capital by some £400m (on the basis of an average turnover of £6.3bn pa. over this period). Since the average for the chemicals sector at that time was, however, a positive 4.49 per cent, the ICI figures were not much out of line with that and as a general judgement, therefore, their monetary working capital seems to have been reasonable in the context of their sector.

### Exchange risk

Exchange exposure is a problem that will only engage the attention of those with a substantial involvement in overseas trade or with investments or borrowing abroad. Exports and imports may be adequately covered by forward buying of currency and insurance, including through the government sponsored export credit guarantee system. These topics are specialized and are not treated here as part of the planning process. What is important for planning, is the limitation of long-term exposure to exchange fluctuations on the values of assets and liabilities.

The general rule should be to cover assets with liabilities (and vice versa) of a roughly comparable amount, so that variations in the rates will have a neutral effect on the business. The point is to try to avoid being involved in currency speculation to any extent. This principle was ignored by many companies in the early 'sixties, before inflation and currency fluctuations became a formidable problem in the UK. In 1963, a balance sheet might have included the following debt which had been raised during the previous financial year:

> 4.5% Swiss loan 1972/77 SwFr.50m (£4.1m at £1 = SwFr.12.2)
> 5.25% Dutch notes 1973/77 DFl.20m (£2.0m at £1 = DFl.10.0)

By 1977, the exchange rates to the £ had moved as shown in Table 10.4. The repayment of these debts would have proved painful.

The seduction of low rates of interest and the availability of funds in a particular country is something to be resisted unless they are matched by profits and assets of broadly similar amounts. Often low rates are an indication of the financial community's expectation of the direction in which exchange rates will

Table 10.4   Exchange rate movements

|  | 1972 | 1973 | 1974 | 1975 | 1976 | 1977 |
|---|---|---|---|---|---|---|
| Swiss Francs | 10.1 | 7.9 | 7.2 | 6.0 | 5.0 | 4.4 |
| Dutch Florins | 8.3 | 7.2 | 6.5 | 5.7 | 5.2 | 4.3 |

move in the future; the lower the rate, the stronger the currency is expected to become.

## Taxation

Tax management is an area which rewards expertise most highly, yet is often neglected in the preparation of plans. While it would be wrong to turn business upside down and change the focus from the market place, none the less the whole planning process involves making trade-off decisions among the various factors which have an influence—whether, for instance, to take the benefit of low-cost raw materials, or to install equipment that requires better materials, but that processes them more efficiently; or whether to trade up or down market with consequent price/volume/mix options. Trade-offs apply equally to decisions affecting taxation, such as the location of a plant in a particular region or country, or the adoption of a particular structure because of favourable fiscal treatment.

In the preparation of plans, the finance manager should be requested to address, from the following matters, those that will have important implications for cash flow, or that may influence a tactical decision on how to go about a particular project:

- VAT and sales taxes;
- customs and excise duties, for example those charged internally such as on fuel or wines and spirits, or those imposed upon imports; the question of local duties on exports are normally dealt with by operating management;
- corporation tax, or, in the case of an individual or partnership, income tax;
- allowances and grants, including those for regional development and those available through the EEC;
- capital gains and, for the individual, capital transfer taxes, where these affect disposal as well as acquisition of assets and businesses;
- exchange controls and withholding taxes which affect remittances to and from overseas.

The object is to maximize the receipt of grants and allowances and to minimize the payment of charges of any nature, within the framework of normal business transactions.

## Distribution policy

If Jack Robinson and his family are the owners of Plinmo, the amount of money that he takes out of the business will be dictated by what he wants, though he will undoubtedly consult his tax adviser on how much he will have to pay the Inland Revenue for the privilege. Even in his case, however, the maximum available will be a question of what funds are required to be retained in the business, as was shown in Figs 9.1 and 9.2.

Where there are other shareholders, however, their personal requirements and tax positions vary from individual to individual. The distribution policy has to depend on other considerations. As a general rule, shareholders will expect to receive the maximum dividend consistent with an adequate re-investment policy. A broad measure of the level of dividend properly payable is earnings cover. This is the number of times that the dividend could be paid out of earnings. The current acceptable level is around the three times mark.

There are exceptions. Companies do try to avoid reducing their pay-out rate. Holding the rate, even in times of poor results, tends to be a corporate virility symbol. It is hoped that its maintenance may help to hold the share price up temporarily and keep the shareholders off the backs of the managers until things can be put right. But poor performance must result in a sagging share price and to try to prop it up by excessive dividend payments is unwise and ineffective. To pay an inadequately covered dividend when there is no end to the problems in sight, diminishes for no good cause the resource available to the business. Cash is handed over to the shareholders and to the government (by way of tax); it will cost much to restore it by alternative borrowings and if the shareholders are asked to chip in again, the part paid over as tax will be a total loss.

If the business is sound, however, there is merit in trying to keep a steady distribution level over time. A one-off dip in profit by reason of a non-recurring problem can be ignored for these purposes. The desirability for a steady rate argues, however, for a reasonably cautious, rather than a generous policy. The press comments on the dividend of Midland Bank when it was embroiled with problems over its US subsidiary, Crocker, are interesting in this context.[5]

### Share price

In addition to income, shareholders are interested in the price at which they may be able to sell their shares. This is also a matter of considerable importance to a business that seeks to undertake an expansion strategy through acquisition (see Chapter 9). One of the most influential factors on price is the level of earnings. It may be significantly influenced by interest and tax as well as by trading performance. This review of the finance plan concludes with a consideration of the issues affecting share price and how different business and financial tactics may affect it.

A recent study of 236 quoted companies on the London Stock Exchange from 1972 to 1981[6] demonstrated that the following were the most important determinants of share price:

- Return on investment—broadly ROTC as defined; this is the most important lever.

- Growth in sales: this was used as a surrogate for earnings growth because of the large number of companies with negative or low earnings. It is an interesting feature of the study that the market seemed to be better at taking account of future growth than at discounting future returns.
- Debt–equity ratio; this is a complex effect. The price appears to decline relative to gearing up to the market average (of around 30 per cent at the time of writing). Gearing above this level tends to push the price up. This seems perverse, but is explained by lack of rights issues (which always depress price) and hopes of good returns following heavy investment or recent acquisitions. Remember, also, that the effects of gearing on the share price are not isolated from all the other factors and high gearing coupled with low earnings would not be a winning combination.
- The overall level of the market at the relevant time. This factor will influence timing of actions, where shares are to be used or an issue is to be made. It is, however, not something that is within the control of the company.

There were some other less dominant factors which, nevertheless, proved to be of some significance, including:

- Dividend pay-out: the message from the statistics bears out what was said in the previous section, that for distributions up to 33 per cent of earnings, the higher the dividend, the better the share price, but dividends over that level have a negative effect.
- Tax rate: the more the government takes, the unhappier investors are.
- Investment intensity: shareholders seem to have more confidence in the continuation of high profit levels if they are generated from a large visible asset base. This is an illogical attitude which does not, nevertheless, inhibit some of the high flying sectors such as business publishing and high tech. service companies from hitting very high ratings. The reason seems to stem from the tendency for financial reporters to focus strongly on profit margin as a performance measure. This ignores the benefits of low capital intensity.

There are a number of other contributory factors, but the above were identified as the main ones to consider when deciding which levers to pull to improve the share price. This information may be used to assess what the price, and hence the PER of individual shares should be, and also to determine the best way of improving the rating of shares to some target PER. The method gives a reasonably good result for normal industrial companies, but there are some that do not conform to the pattern. This indicates that there must be other influences which have not been captured by the analysis. It could, of course, be random differences, but there are some pointers to other factors.

Consider the share prices of three conglomerates shown in Table 10.5 (conglomerates are chosen because they spread across a variety of different industrial and commercial sectors and this should diminish the influence of any

**Table 10.5**   Conglomerate share prices

|        | Market price | Price by analysis |
|--------|--------------|-------------------|
| BTR    | £4.89        | £3.23             |
| BET    | £2.63        | £2.45             |
| Lonrho | £1.44        | £2.22             |

potential sectoral differences). These figures were calculated in September 1984. BTR was well above its par rating as given by the anaylsis, BET was more or less in line, while Lonrho was well below.

A number of explanations have been proposed of which at least three seem plausible. These are that the market responds favourably to

- low volatility in year by year earnings;
- a low-profile, professional style of management rather than a flamboyant, personalized image;
- investment in what are perceived to be relatively low political risk regions.

The respective patterns of earnings growth of the three examples are shown in the graph in Fig. 10.1.[7] This demonstrates the relative volatilities of the earnings of the three groups. Lonrho over the relevant period showed the greatest fluctuations, though BET showed some downturns as well as upturns. Only BTR maintained a consistently upward movement. As to the other two points, Owen Green of BTR and Tiny Rowlands of Lonrho are both tough, well-known leaders, but the latter adopts a much more public image at times.

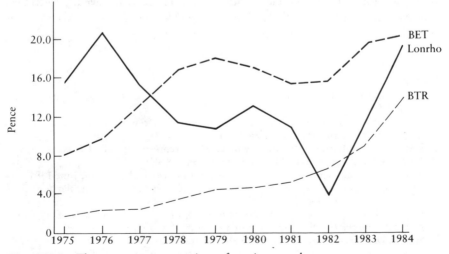

**Figure 10.1**   Three-company comparison of earnings per share

Furthermore, Lonrho has substantially more investments in territories that may be thought of as more risk prone than has BTR. Though none of these explanations has been substantiated statistically, they are intuitively persuasive and seem likely to contribute to the different ratings that BTR and Lonrho have, compared to the par ratings indicated by the analysis.

Within the limiting factor of the state of the stock market at any given time, therefore, the levers to pull to make a change in share rating have been identified as:

- level of profit
- growth
- gearing
- dividend pay-out
- tax rate
- investment intensity

and perhaps one or all of the following:

- earnings volatility
- managerial profile
- perceived political risk

Achieving an improved rating is a slow process. Since the share price depends primarily on increasing profits and earnings, it must be thought of as part of the strategic programme, to be fulfilled over a period of years rather than months. It pays, nevertheless, to let the financial community know what is going on as early as sensible commercial confidentiality allows. The market will respond to the perception that the right measures are being taken, even though the full potential rating may be withheld until success has been achieved. Sometimes, however, the market is a little hard of hearing. The message may have to be repeated again and again and at the top of the voice!

## Notes

1. For a brief description, see 'Unlisted securities market', *Financial Times Survey*, *Financial Times*, London, 30 January 1985.
2. *The Equity Book*, produced annually by Phillips & Drew, stockbrokers, London, gives a variety of information on such ratios.
3. See, for example, 'How to be a winner with venture capital', *Chemical Week*, McGraw-Hill, New York, 14 December 1983, pp. 38–43.
4. Source: the *Datastream Database*, Datastream International, London, June 1984.
5. See Press comment from December 1983 to March 1985 and in particular *Financial Times*, London, 29 June 1984.
6. K. J. Roberts, *Research on the Determinants of Stock Market Valuations of Companies within the UK*, Strategic Planning Institute, London, 1982.
7. Source: Datastream International, London, September 1984.

# 11

# The planning machine

The previous chapters have described the components of a planning system—
what is necessary, through a proper consideration of the various factors, to
produce plans that move the business towards its ojectives in a reasonably practical and robust way. Part 1 now concludes with an assembly manual, where all
the pieces are fitted together and the complete machine emerges. The parts are
given a visual coding as shown in Fig. 11.1 on page 112.

The first set of components, discussed in Chapter 3, comprised the structure
of business generally as set out in Fig. 11.2.

Almost all organizations are concerned with a number of markets, some of
which may intersect either on the supply or the demand side. Plinmo is engaged
in several markets: if it were limited to two, the business cluster could be represented by the diagram in Fig. 11.3 on page 113. For a larger number of markets,
the diagram has to be generalized to enable it to be fitted into the whole structure. It is shortened, therefore, into the picture shown in Fig. 11.4 which serves
to represent the full complexity described above.

The business itself may be translated into profit and loss account, balance
sheet and so on (see Chapter 3). When enriched with information about
markets, locations, personnel and production, it forms a data base that can be
organized as a model to simulate the structure and dynamics of the business. It
is largely described in financial terms, since this is the language of business. It is
this model called 'FINMOD' (short for 'financial model') which lies at the core
of the planning system.

Strategic changes will affect the structure of the business (Chapter 5). These
are implemented through tactical moves (Chapter 7). Both the strategy and tactics lead to the finance plan (Chapter 10). FINMOD may be used to test the implications of strategic tactical or financial proposals, before implementation,
for example:

- What would be the effect of growing business A faster, selling business B,
  acquiring business C?
- What would happen if the business were to adopt a different pricing policy,
  higher working capital, more fixed capital expenditure?
- How would gearing be affected by an acquisition for shares, a change in taxation, further borrowings?

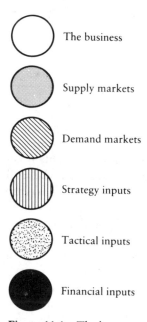

The business

Supply markets

Demand markets

Strategy inputs

Tactical inputs

Financial inputs

**Figure 11.1**    The key

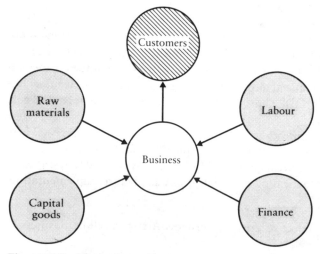

**Figure 11.2**    The business cluster

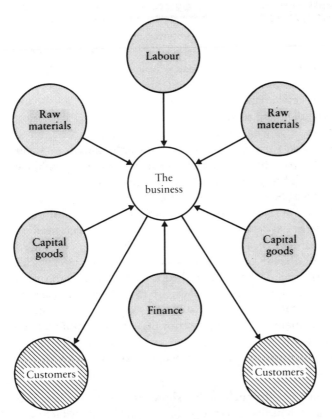

**Figure 11.3**    An extended business cluster

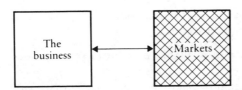

**Figure 11.4**    The business cluster symbolized

The arrows in the diagram in Fig. 11.5 indicate this interactive planning process by pointing in both directions.

Obviously, if FINMOD is to be used effectively in this interactive way in a large group, it has to be constructed as a computer model, though the procedure can be followed, if rather more laboriously, by working through the figures with a calculator and a wet towel. Whatever method is adopted, tentative plans may be tried out and finally the best one may be selected. This becomes the formally accepted plan for the business.

Retreating a step, the planning process started with base-case assumptions about the environment within which the business was operating (Chapter 8). This influenced strategies only to a limited extent, but was an important determinant of tactics and, in terms of interest and exchange rates, was a vital element of the financial plan. This component is represented in Fig 11.6.

The base-case scenario is, however, only an informed guess and alternatives are reviewed, using models of the macroeconomic environment and of the individual markets in which the business is operating. Again, these models need not be computer simulations, though it is easier to follow the process through if they are. The impact of change on the key assumptions as to interest and exchange rates and costs and sales can be studied and then tested out on the business (FINMOD), to see how robust the plans are to such changes (see Fig. 11.7 on page 116). The feedback from FINMOD to scenarios represents the link necessary to help the planners design scenarios that are relevant and likely to have a significant impact.

From these various processes emerge a number of outputs, via FINMOD, including the following:

- *Strategic*    market share profiles such as that shown in Fig. 11.8. These profiles provide goals for each business sector within which to plan its tactics.
- *Tactical* – price/volume data
              – capacity utilization/productivity indices
              – ROTC, growth and other targets
- *Financial* – profit and loss, balance sheet, cash flow
              – D–E ratio
              – EPS
- *Environmental* – market growth: a similar histogram to that in Fig. 11.8 or a graph could be produced for each market sector.

The above is only a sample of the outputs available; each business should design what it needs for itself.

The various parts of the machine are now ready to be put together (see Fig. 11.9 on page 117). One vital feature has not been included. That is the objectives. They rarely change, yet they influence everything else and pervade the whole system—at least until some corporate Calvin comes along and leads commercial man along a new path. The objectives cannot be adequately

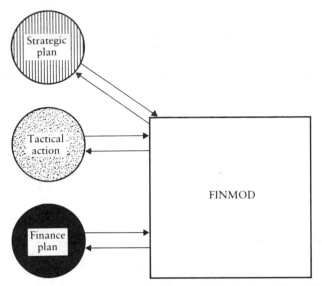

**Figure 11.5**    Structure, tactics, finance and the financial model

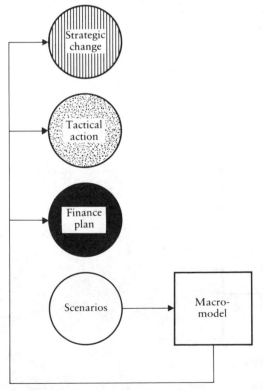

**Figure 11.6**    Structure, tactics, finance and environmental change

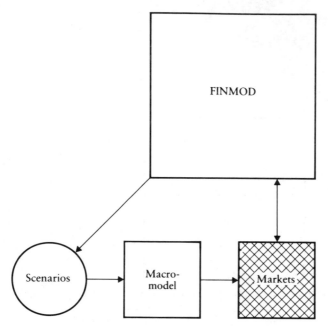

**Figure 11.7**    Scenarios and the financial model

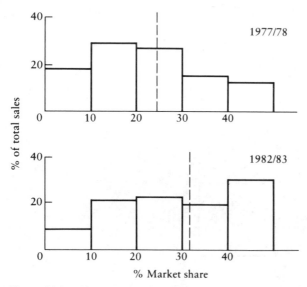

**Figure 11.8**    Change in market share

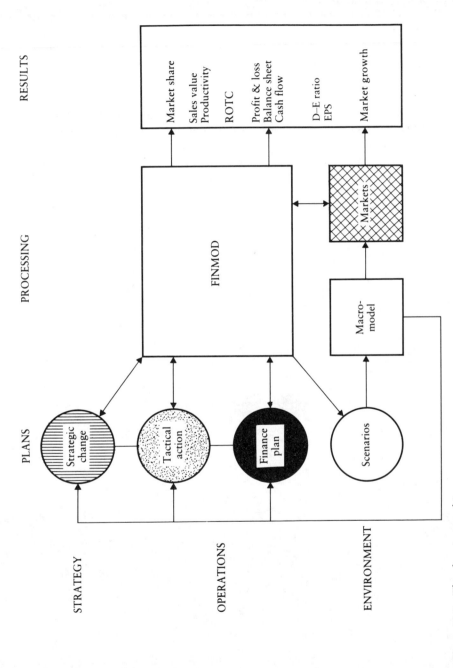

**Figure 11.9**    The planning machine

represented in the illustration, but·they are very much there, providing the focus without which corporate life would be aimless.

This apart, therefore, the diagram provides a blueprint for the whole planning machine. The labels across the top indicate the parts devoted to inputs, to processing and to outputs. It divides horizontally into strategic, operational and environmental matters. It is not a magic black box. It only sets out a systematic way for thinking through the plans of a business. The degree of analysis undertaken for each part and the mechanisms employed will vary substantially from business to business. Each stage is, nevertheless, important and should be gone through in as much detail as the responsible and informed manager considers appropriate.

# PART 2
# The management of planning

Part 1 was concerned with the concepts of planning and the reason why the various components were included in the planning machine. Part 2 is concerned with the management of planning and how to operate the machine. While the various components described in Part 1 are all necessary for the production of effective plans, the way in which the machine is driven is much less determined by theory.

There are, indeed, as many different ways to plan as there are commercial organizations. There is no one right way. It depends on many factors such as the markets in which the business operates, the cultural and legal frameworks and the time-scales which dominate the markets. For instance, the construction and subsequent running in to profit of a paper mill will take over seven years. On the other hand, a newspaper is one of the most perishable products there is and, as a result, the operating horizons are very short-term, normally around 24 hours. While their strategy plans have to be rather more prolonged, there is always a tendency to take the quick view. In addition to this, both businesses are involved in the political scene, newspapers because of what they report and comment, and paper as a strategic material. All these factors add up to the reality that those businesses will be conducted on very different lines and this will be even more different if one is in, say, Brazil and the other is in Canada.

These differences are important, but there is one even more critical element. The way in which a business actually undertakes its planning depends decisively on the people involved, their attitudes, their personal goals and their experience.

This discussion of the management of planning will outline some of the ways in which planning has been successfully undertaken in the past, but it cannot lay down a blueprint of how to do it with anything like the degree of certainty that attaches to the structure of the system described in Part 1. The style for each business must be left to the manager who takes on this responsibility.

# 12

# Information gathering

## Information sources

The raw material for planning is information. There are plenty of yahoos in the commercial world, ready to jeer at an automated planning system and cry: 'Garbage in, garbage out'! Unhappily, they are right, even though they may not have sufficient wit to understand fully their own gibe. If bad information is fed into the computerized planning machine it cannot transform it into good. It may be able to detect some defects and perhaps identify inconsistencies. It is, however, undoubtedly less able to detect garbage than is an experienced operator. This puts a premium on ensuring that what is fed in is correct—and this means that the intervention of experienced managers is a critical element in the total system.

Computers are acknowledged to be better than humans at performing complex algorithmic functions, that is those for which there is a set method for calculating the required solution. This implies that having constructed a computerized system such as FINMOD, the future emphasis of the accountant's task will be less on compiling figures and more on the audit of data. The accountant will be required to ascertain, as far as possible, that the information is relevant, accurate, consistent and complete. Of course he or she will still be required to press the buttons to extract information in given formats, but this latter function is one which technology is rapidly deskilling.

Information selection and the application to data of the four criteria mentioned above is, however, far from becoming automated, though some part of the information gathering process is computerized. The main reason why human skill remains important is the difficulty of designing a system that meets the needs of every different user. Allied to this is the enormous number of sources.

Sources may be categorized as follows:

- *formal*   – strategic and tactical plans
            – periodic internal business reports
            – *ad hoc* studies
- *informal*  – the media
            – internal networks
            – external advisors

– trade associations
– customer contacts

This list is by no means exhaustive, but it serves as an example of some of the more important items.

Before considering these sources in more depth, it has to be emphasized again that, as in all other aspects of planning, it is essential to organize the information gathering process to conform to market requirements, rather than, for example, those of production. The focus must be the served market (see Chapter 5). The 'strategic business unit' is the term used by a number of commentators such as Boston Consulting Group and the Strategic Planning Institute, to describe a business devoted to a particular served market, and in the examples which follow, the individual units are referred to as 'SBUs'.

## Strategic plans

Turning now to the first of the sources mentioned, the instructions to those preparing a strategic plan comprise a key element. Two different types of instructions, indicating the sort of information to be provided for strategic purposes are reproduced below.

### Alternative 1

#### Strategic plan 19—

The following schedules, once completed, provide a numerate summary of your preferred strategies and the principal tactics envisaged to accomplish them in respect of each of your SBUs. The forms should be fully completed for each SBU and accompanied by a brief statement of your intentions. They will be read in conjunction with the financial schedules submitted on ...............; if there are any *major* changes expected since those schedules were submitted, they should be prepared again and sent in with your strategy schedules.

Your plans will be considered at a review meeting on ............... when the various market options will be discussed. If you wish to propose alternative strategies, they should be included as a complete additional set, explaining the circumstances under which the alternatives would be preferred.

| Business • • • • • • • • • • • | 77/8 | 82/3 | 87/8 | Accuracy |
|---|---|---|---|---|
| **Performance** | | | | |
| Profit/sales (%) | ☐☐☐ | ☐☐☐ | ☐☐☐ | (± 0.5% points) |
| Return on trading capital (%) | | | | (± 0.5% points) |
| Index of total sales at 76/7 prices (volume) | | | | (± 1) |
| **Market stance and competitive position** | | | | |
| Index of underlying market growth | ☐☐☐☐ | ☐☐☐☐ | ☐☐☐☐ | (± 1) |
| Index of market breadth | | | | (± 1) |
| Market share (%) | | | | (± 2% points) |
| Index of growth in market penetration by acquisition | | | | (± 1) |
| **Productivity** | | | | |
| Index value added per employee at constant prices | ☐☐ | ☐☐ | ☐☐ | (± 1) |
| Value added/£ of wages and salaries | | | | (± 5p) |
| **Vertical integration** | | | | |
| Backward vertical integration (%) | ☐ | ☐ | ☐ | (± 2% points) |

**Figure 12.1**   Summary schedule: principal ratios

Business . . . . . . . . . . . . .

| | | 74/5 | 77/8 | 80/1 | Accuracy |
|---|---|---|---|---|---|
| Marketing expenditure | | ☐☐☐ | ☐ | ☐☐☐ | |
| % of end-users by sales Volume who consider your products | Superior | | ☐ | ☐ | |
| | Equivalent | | ☐ | ☐ | (± 5% points) |
| | Inferior | | ☐ | ☐ | |
| Selling price index relative to leading competitors (100 = same) | | | ☐ | ☐ | (± 1% points) |
| % of sales accounted for by new products introduced in three preceding years | This business | | ☐ | ☐ | (± 1% points) |
| | Leading competitors | | ☐ | ☐ | |

**Figure 12.2** Schedule A: market stance

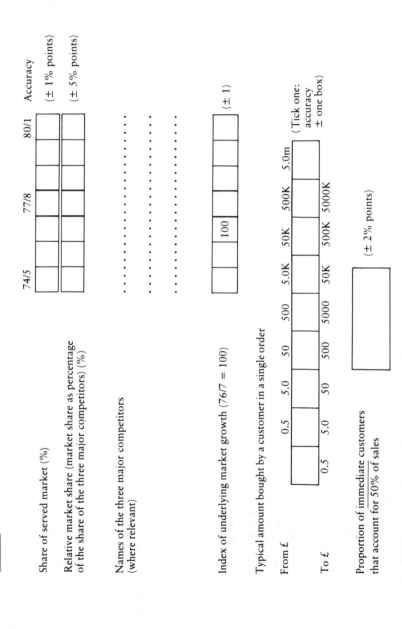

**Figure 12.3**    Schedule B: market data and competitive position

Business . . . . . . . . . . . . . . . .

Index of direct costs per unit relative to leading competitors (100 = same)

Index of wage (and salary) levels relative to leading competitors (100 = same)

Relative to its leading competitors is the vertical integration of this business

Backward — More / Same / Less

Forward — More / Same / Less

77/8     80/1     Accuracy

(± 1)

(± 1)

Tick one

Tick one

**Figure 12.4** Schedule C: relative production and cost advantages

All this information is concerned with ways in which the SBU may achieve competitive advantage. The second approach is of a very different character.

### Alternative 2

#### Strategic plan 19—

*Guidelines on plan content*

### General

Detailed figures are to be supplied in the schedules attached to these guidelines. The important part of your plan, however, is your description of your strategies which should be as full as is necessary to explain what you wish to achieve. In preparing this, you are not bound to use the headings listed below, nor are they an exhaustive list. These are suggestions only and are intended to guide your thinking.

### Current activities and outlook for the future

- Define the SBU you are in, its boundaries and your position in the market.
- What is the competition (including competitive products and imports)? Will this intensify?
- What product development or technological change may occur?
- What are the prospects for growth within your served markets?
- How do your production facilities, processes and capacity utilization match the industry?
- What strengths or weaknesses underpin or undermine the quality of your profit and the security of your profit generating base?

### Environment

- What external factors affect the activity, such as:
  - raw materials, supplier relationships
  - industrial relations
  - economic trends and fluctuations in exchange rates
  - government legislation
  - customer industries
- What will affect the level of supply and demand in the market?
- The schedule following these guidelines includes specific cost headings. How will these and other major costs in your supply markets move?
- To what extent will prices and margins for your products respond to changes in these external factors?

### Strategies

The strategies that you wish to adopt may be stated in the alternative, but the preferred option must be made clear.

- Indicate the realistic alternatives open for the development of each SBU and state your preferred strategy.
- State your consequent business goals and the logic for them. Goals may be in part qualitative, such as reputation, market stance or product range, or quantitative e.g. market share.
- In the long run, what products will you sell in your served markets and what products in new markets?
- What events may necessitate a rethink?

### Tactics

These items indicate the feasibility of your strategic goals and at this stage are not treated as a commitment. They may be stated in the alternative, though the preferred course should always be made clear.

- How is the strategy to be implemented?
- What are the key action or decision areas? These may cover sales and marketing, capital, production facilities, product development, R&D, acquisitions, divestments, rationalization.
- What additional resources are required, such as management, production, financial? What capital expenditure is proposed and what will be the benefit of such investment?
- What risks are there; what is the 'upside' and 'downside' potential?
- How will the market or competition react?

### Financial outcome

This review is primarily concerned with the presentation of strategies and goals. The figures on the attached schedule* may be broad, perhaps speculative, but are needed to put the strategy in context. It is left to you to decide what further relevant information may be useful to clarify any figures stated. Comments are required on trends in items such as value added, profitability, margins, returns and cash flow.

THE ALTERNATIVES COMPARED
The above two alternatives describe two different approaches to information gathering. The first is basically statistical. It represents a sophisticated approach, where changes in ratios imply changes in some important feature of management action. Thus, if materially increased values are simultaneously projected for sales volumes and for value added per employee, but very little else changes, this means that some major rise in market share is expected through operating efficiencies and consequent competitive advantage. The specific tactics to be employed will be ascertained at a subsequent review meeting. Such an approach avoids the use of a lot of words, but means that the readers

*This will be similar to the activity schedule shown in Appendix 2

have to be astute to pick up the various nuances in the numbers. It is probably most useful in an organization such as Conglom which has a widely differing set of businesses and a large number of individual activities to deal with. It needs a skilled staff to assist in interpretation.

Plinmo would probably prefer the second, more literate approach. This requires managers to set down in some detail their thinking about the business. It has the advantage that it requires a fairly full statement of the business and its environment and rehearses the managers in the options they have available. Note that the distinction between strategies and tactics becomes blurred in these documents. While the strategy plan concentrates on the market factors, it still requires some fleshing out in tactical terms, though at the strategic stage these may be purely tentative.

## Operating plans

Operating plans (i.e. those dealing with tactics and finance) should not go over the strategies again though they may be restated with the specific goals. The main focus of operating plans is to indicate in detail and with commitment, how the business is going to achieve those goals.

The following text sets out instructions for information gathering for operating plans. In this case, there is little difference between the Conglom and Plinmo approaches.

### ANNUAL BUSINESS PLAN INSTRUCTIONS 19—

**1. General**

1.1 An annual plan, based upon the strategies agreed at the strategy review in Autumn 19—, will be prepared for each SBU in accordance with the following general guidelines.

1.2 The plan will cover the year 19—, and include comparative information in respect of last year's plan and latest estimate for the current year. The latest estimate included in the plan document must agree in all respects with the Period 10 latest estimate submitted as part of the monthly reports. At the time of the plan review, each SBU will confirm or modify its latest estimate.

1.3 The SBUs required to report are specified in Appendix A hereto [not included in this example].

**2. Plan text**

The text should concentrate on specifics as follows:

2.1 A statement of performance targets and comments relating particularly to:

- Volumes and prices of major product lines

- Relative market share (including expectations for major competitors)
- Cost escalation for materials and wages
- Productivity (however measured)
- Overheads and non-operational items

The above will include a statement of factors upon which their achievement will depend.

2.2    Commentary on:

- Capital expenditure, including indications of the extent to which this expands capacity and relates to planned sales volumes
- Major additions to working capital; control levels adopted
- Acquisitions
- Disposals/closures

2.3    Management action benchmarks. These will be as reasonably explicit as possible, to give timing as well as a statement of the specific actions proposed.

2.4    Management, manpower and industrial relations:

- Organization
- Industrial relations
- Personnel policy issues

The foregoing lists represent an indication of topics to be covered. It need not be followed in detail (or in any specific order). What is important is that the key targets by which performance may be judged should be stated and explained.

**3. Plan schedules**

These are to be in the form set out in Appendix B hereto. [Appendix 2 in this book.]

The above minimal instructions set out what is basically required for the business plans and each business will elaborate on these. A most important part of the exercise, however, is the detailed information provided in the schedules.


## Other internal reports

Reports against plan are considered in detail in Chapter 16. These are a vital source of information. The only point to make at this stage is that plans are normally based on an estimate for the current year. When the results for the year have been finally completed, the estimate and the actual are often significantly different in some respects. This is particularly true of cash flow and the working capital elements. The cash flow, for example, may have swelled the corporate pool less than expected and the manager, poised on his springboard to launch into the future, ought to know this as soon as possible to avoid diving into the mud. The tactical and finance plans may need early adjustment; this means that the correct information should be substituted in them as soon as it is available. It is a frequent feature of plans that last year's figures never get corrected until the next planning round, perhaps a year later. It is a gap in the system which ought to be plugged.

### External reports

Formal reports available to the organization from external sources cover an immense number of topics. These are produced through a wide variety of agencies in many different forms. Table 12.1 sets out a sample.

**Table 12.1**    External reports

| Agency | Format | Subject |
|---|---|---|
| Batelle Institute | Newsletter | R&D and technology news |
| CBI | Quarterly reports | Business trends |
| CSO Business Monitor | Books/floppy discs | Industry sector information |
| Data Resources Inc. | Database/books | Economic information |
| Extel | Cards | Company accounts and shares |
| Kompass Register | Directory | Company products/services |

Bespoke reports on any specific business topic are available through a wide variety of management consultants. The Marketing Surveys Index[1] is just one of a number of directories of market research information published to business users generally. There are, also, other agencies such as Dialog or Infoline[2] which give information on or access to a wide spectrum of data bases.

### Informal sources

Gossip is a fruitful, but hazardous source of information. So often the chat goes round the market place that so-and-so is in trouble and is not likely to survive. The members of Fleet Street at one time were continually forecasting the imminent demise of their competitors on the flimsiest of evidence. Many of the targets of such rumours still survive—though it is certainly true that some of them have been at times in dire financial straits. It is essential, therefore, that gossip should be thoroughly checked before it can be trusted as a basis for action. This is all part of the data audit referred to earlier, but in the case of information that is whispered, rather than published with the author's name, the lack of responsibility from its source must make it more suspect.

On the other hand, the manager who does not swap news over the village pump is going to miss a lot of what is going on. The supplier of equipment or raw materials, anxious to sell to others, will try to reinforce the image of his products by telling how many he has sold and to whom. The labour side of the business may be explored by reading the situations vacant columns in the press and by talking to employment agencies. Lawyers, bankers, estate agents and other external advisers—provided they do not act for the competition—are other useful sources of information. A fair picture of rival firms can be constructed.

Mingling with the opposition directly is another important activity. The question 'How's business?' should be directed to trying to find out something important rather than a mere social pleasantry. It is surprising how much people are prepared to divulge, particularly over a convivial jar at a trade association dinner or chamber of commerce lunch. Cocktail hour at a seminar (especially if the proceedings have been dull) is another good place to exchange yarns.

Snippets of information from the local or national press or trade magazines give useful hints on changes in the competitors' management or production facilities and in contracts available and awarded. Sales brochures are direct evidence of the product lines offered and the prices being charged—though it may be a little more difficult to find out the real prices paid after discounts and allowances are taken into account. If needs be, some goods could be purchased, to test this and also quality and service. Trade shows can also be important: the products emphasized by rival firms, the customers they are courting and the standard of efficiency and display at such events are further important clues.

A most important source of information on the market must, however, be a well-trained and alert sales force. They will feed back a mass of data such as how many bars of Galaxy or Cadbury's chocolate are on display, which tractor manufacturers were represented at the Bath and Wells agricultural show, and what discounts are being offered on the new range of Sierra motor cars. How much their own business sells is vital information, but it is almost as critical to know what the opposition is doing and whether the market is growing, static or diminishing.

In the end, managers best equipped for beating the competition are those who have the best information, so that, should they choose to do so, they could even write a business plan for their principle rivals. An executive of United Technology in the USA, the company that manufactures Pratt and Whitney aero-engines, related once that when the Chairman of Rolls-Royce was visiting from the UK, he was presented by his opposite number with a business plan for Rolls-Royce to flick through. 'How did you manage to get hold of this?' exclaimed the Chairman with some concern. 'We wrote it!' was the answer.

## Notes

1. *Marketing Surveys Index* is published annually by Marketing Strategies for Industry, in association with the Institute of Marketing.
2. Infoline is the data base service of Pergamon Press, Oxford and Dialog is managed in the UK by Lockheed Dialog Retrieval Service, Oxford.

# 13

# Using information

## The use of information

There are some corporate headquarters that suffer from the boa constrictor syndrome.[1] They call for an immense amount of information which they swallow whole. The organization remains comatose as the headquarters goes through the process of data digestion which never really ends. The small business is fortunate that it cannot afford the luxury of a large staff which might indulge in such a gourmand approach. The principle to follow, however, whatever the size of organization, is that no information should be demanded (or supplied) on a routine basis unless it can be, and frequently is, purposefully used.

Furthermore, it should also be the aim that the reason why the information is required should be understood by those providing it, as well as those seeking it. A recognition of what it is for can improve appreciably the quality of the data—provided both sides are following the same business aims.

This is an important proviso. It is the job of the chief executive to install managers who are dedicated to the same corporate objectives, but a strong local manager may want to get there by a different strategic route. This can result in all sorts of data dust storms and information side-tracks. In order to combat this managerial desert warfare, chief executives, either themselves, or through their aides, must be competent in analysing the information provided by their managers.

## Techniques for analysis

This introduces the subject of techniques for analysis, ranging from the very simple to the highly sophisticated. The following pages discuss a number of these as listed in Table 13.1 to give a flavour of the very wide spectrum of methods that are available and the occasions when they may be suitable in assisting in the planning process.

## Matrices

A matrix is a grid of information, normally in two dimensions, where some characteristic of a business is measured by reference to two different factors.

**Table 13.1**    Analytical techniques

| | |
|---|---|
| ● Matrices | – two dimensional |
| | – directional policy |
| ● Curves | – experience |
| | – maturity |
| ● Delphi method | |
| ● Spreadsheets | – e.g. VisiCalc, Lotus 1–2–3 |
| ● Trend analysis | – Simple time trend |
| | – multiple regressions |
| | – model building |
| ● Cross-sectional analysis | – PIMS |
| ● Expert systems | |

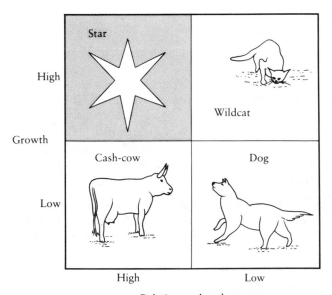

**Figure 13.1**    The growth/share matrix

The most famous is that popularized by the Boston Consulting Group. This rates the cash flow of a business according to growth and market share.

In the matrix in Fig. 13.1:

- high growth, high share businesses are the stars, with a good positive cash flow;
- high growth, low share businesses are the wildcats which are generally in an

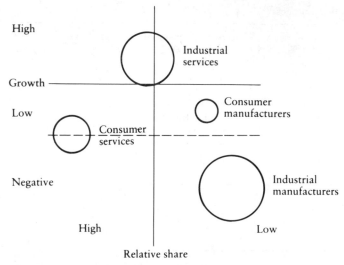

**Figure 13.2**    Conglom's businesses 1980

early stage of development, hopefully to become stars: they tend to absorb cash;

- high share, low growth businesses are cash-cows which provide money to finance other businesses in the portfolio;
- low share, low growth businesses are the dogs which often have a negative cash flow and no prospects.

These sorts of diagrams may be developed to give a snapshot of all the businesses in the company's portfolio, or of all the competition in a particular market place. In Fig. 13.2, which illustrates Conglom's businesses, a third dimension is added through the size of the circles drawn. The larger the size of the circle, the larger the relative size of the business concerned, its point on the grid being fixed by reference to its centre. Note, however, that this third dimension is only an added piece of information and is not shown to be related to the other two in any way.

The above method provides a useful start in looking at various aspects of the business. It has, however, necessary drawbacks, resulting from the simplicity of the approach:

- first, the matrix can only be a snapshot in time and does not show the direction in which a business is going;
- second, the lines in the matrix are drawn arbitrarily; at what level of growth or share should a business be considered a star or a dog?
- third, matrices are limited to two or, at the most, three characteristics and do

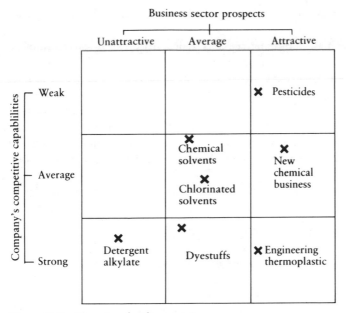

**Figure 13.3**    Directional policy matrix

not capture other influences which are affecting the business at the same time (e.g., capital intensity).

Some of these disadvantages may be reduced, for example by adopting dimensions which reflect a dynamic, such as the rate of growth of the business, or how fast it is losing share. The matrix could be enlarged to say 3 × 3 or 4 × 4 to reduce the arbitrariness of the subdivisions. A matrix of more than 16 squares, however, is likely to be too complex visually to help in presenting a clear picture of the chosen characteristic.

DIRECTIONAL POLICY MATRICES

The usefulness of this type of diagram was enhanced by the development of the directional policy matrix (DPM) by Shell to assist in the placing of businesses in order of strategic preference.[2] A sample is given in Fig. 13.3.

It is clear from the top and side headings in the diagram that this particular matrix conceals a considerable amount of preparatory work which had to be undertaken before it could be constructed. Characteristics such as 'business sector prospects' are themselves usefully derived from an assembly of other supporting grids of the various important features of the business sector. It can, therefore, be a rather protracted process if all the critical characteristics are matched against one another, as they have to be compared one against one. Furthermore, it is by no means certain whether such characteristics in sets of more than two dimensions at a time would always point to the same conclusions.

For example, if high marketing costs as a proportion of sales are allied to high product quality and a dominant share, this normally indicates a strong competitive position. If, however, to these is added market life cycle, it becomes evident that high marketing to sales will tend to reduce profitability in a very mature market and increase it in a fast growing one. The case of electric showers referred to earlier, bears this out. On the other hand, high product quality fits effectively with a mature market while (within limits) it cuts profit potential in a fast growing one. This sort of problem is tackled by cross-sectional analysis, discussed later.

The following are some of the dimensions along which DPMs have been used effectively:

- Market attractiveness
  - rate of growth
  - maturity level
  - extent of competition
  - cost of entry
  - political risk
- Product attractiveness
  - quality (how tight a specification)
  - differentiation
  - importance to customer
  - size of order

There are many others and some tend to be only reinforcing. Thus, product quality and importance to customers may be alternative ways of viewing the same charateristic; the more important to the customers, the more likely they are to be fussy about the product offered. This is not entirely so, but obviously there is little point in testing one factor against another once such a connection has been demonstrated. In such a case, one of the factors may be used as a surrogate for the other.

A PRACTICAL EXAMPLE

Plinmo might wish to produce a matrix of the last three characteristics referred to above. First, it ranks the importance of its products to customers, say, on a scale of 1–9. It then applies the differentiation test: to what extent is the product like all others offered in the market place, or is it made to the client's specification? The more bespoke it is, the higher the rating. Finally, the normal size of order for each particular brand it produces is ascertained and given a scale value. Table 13.2 illustrates the approach.

Plotted on the matrix, the data in Table 13.2 would appear as in Fig. 13.4, the size of the circles being proportional to the size of the orders. This indicates that two of the product lines are critical to the customer and are designed to

Table 13.2   Product attractiveness factors

| Unit | Importance to customers | Differentiation | Size of order |
|------|------------------------|-----------------|---------------|
| A | 6 | 2 | £1000–£1500 (4) |
| B | 9 | 8 | £200–£500  (2) |
| C | 2 | 3 | £2000–£3000 (6) |
| D | 4 | 4 | £1000–£1500 (4) |
| E | 8 | 7 | £1500–£2000 (5) |

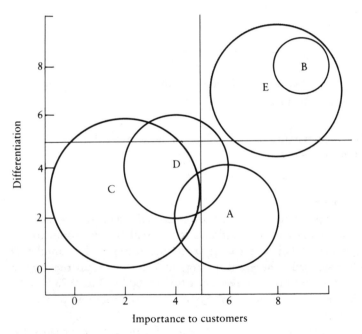

Figure 13.4   Plinmo's products

meet their specification. Two others are run-of-the-mill products, one of which is unimportant to the customer and the fifth is in a middle position.

What does this mean? One possible interpretation is that products B and E are the most attractive for development and that product C is of doubtful benefit to the future of the business. The particular interpretation of this case is, however, unimportant. What is useful is to see how a structuring of information about different features of product lines may help to clarify which are the

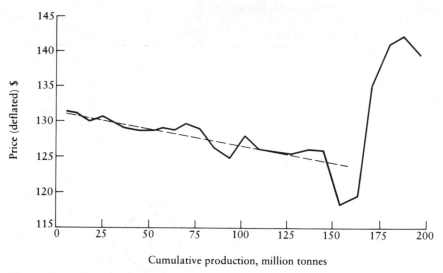

Cumulative production, million tonnes

**Figure 13.5**    Newsprint 1953–1978

ones most likely to achieve success and which are those that will require justification for continued investment.

### The experience curve

This technique, again popularized by the Boston Consulting Group, is based on the proposition that prices and costs fall at a steady real rate in proportion to accumulated experience.[3] This latter is normally measured as the cumulative volume of goods produced. The graph in Fig. 13.5 demonstrates the way in which Canadian newsprint prices moved over the period 1953 to 1978.[4] There is a clear reduction in price as a function of cumulative production up to about the 150 million tonnes mark.

Since paper is a strategic material, the influence of major political events distorts the picture. This is particularly true of the last few observations which represent what happened when the first oil crisis struck. Immediately prior to that, the price of newsprint had fallen significantly, such as to give rise to expectations among users of the experience curve analysis that it would recover quite sharply. The extent to which it reacted was, however, like almost all other commodity price rises, dramatic and alarming. The story could be taken to the present time to show whether prices have again fallen back to the level indicated by the trend; this analysis has not yet been done, but a quick look at the evidence indicates that this is likely.

The moral of the tale is that, given this sort of analysis, managers can come to a view whether the prices of the product they are concerned with are likely to go up or down. Where the graph shows a dip below the trend, this indicates that there is room for an uplift; where it is above, there is likely to be a downward movement. They may not be able to forecast with accuracy when it will happen, but for the purposes of preparing or approving a capital expenditure proposal, for example, they can take a view on the longer-term robustness of the project against such a background. Projects to increase capacity utilization at a time when the price is significantly above the trend, as at the 200 point on the graph in Fig. 13.5, must be suspect; equally, it would be premature to close a plant solely because prices were around those shown against the 150 mark.

Trends can, however, only demonstrate the likely future of a system whose structure does not change. An expectation that the prices of mechanical watches would recover to experience trend levels, after the onslaught of digital timepieces would have been totally misplaced. The recognition that products have a life cycle as well as an experience curve led other commentators to see this particular line developing in a totally different way.

THE MATURITY CURVE
The concept of the maturity curve is that every product has a life cycle, starting with invention and development to commercial launch, proceeding then to early stage, fast development and moving from there to maturity, and ultimately, to decline. The way to manage a business is dependent on the point in this cycle that the business has reached. The diagram in Fig. 13.6 adapts a representation by the Arthur D. Little organization and describes the main principles.[5]

The classification represents archetypes and must, therefore, be treated with caution in individual cases. Nevertheless, it is useful as general guidance to the manager of a number of different units in helping him or her to decide how each of them is going to be run. It will also serve the manager of any one of them to get a view on whether the right sort of approach is being applied in every respect. It is not uncommon for an executive, put in charge of an ageing business, to try to adopt strategies of growth, while administrators are sometimes put in charge of pioneer businesses.

# Delphi method

A technique of a different character is called the Delphi method.[6] This requires the setting up of a panel of experts in a particular area, which could be as narrow as next year's trends in wallcoverings design in the UK, or as wide as the most likely new technologies to be brought into normal world production by the year 2000. Each panel member is requested to state his or her view on the subject in writing. The results are then classified by the sponsors of the research and details of all the responses received are published to the whole group. The panellists are then invited to reconsider their own views in the light of this.

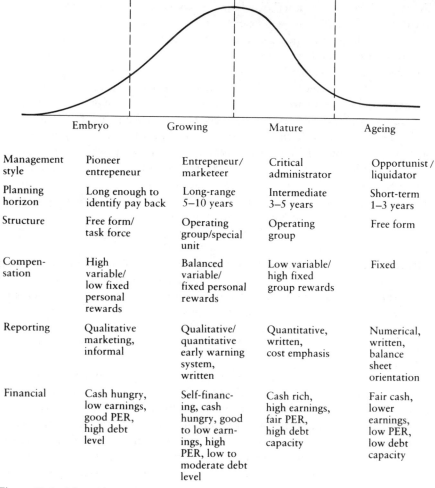

|  | Embryo | Growing | Mature | Ageing |
|---|---|---|---|---|
| Management style | Pioneer entrepeneur | Entrepeneur/ marketeer | Critical administrator | Opportunist / liquidator |
| Planning horizon | Long enough to identify pay back | Long-range 5–10 years | Intermediate 3–5 years | Short-term 1–3 years |
| Structure | Free form/ task force | Operating group/special unit | Operating group | Free form |
| Compen- sation | High variable/ low fixed personal rewards | Balanced variable/ fixed personal rewards | Low variable/ high fixed group rewards | Fixed |
| Reporting | Qualitative marketing, informal | Qualitative/ quantitative early warning system, written | Quantitative, written, cost emphasis | Numerical, written, balance sheet orientation |
| Financial | Cash hungry, low earnings, good PER, high debt level | Self-financ- ing, cash hungry, good to low earn- ings, high PER, low to moderate debt level | Cash rich, high earnings, fair PER, high debt capacity | Fair cash, lower earnings, low PER, low debt capacity |

**Figure 13.6**   Maturity curve

Ultimately, a spectrum of views is produced which has been refined by this iter-
ative process. These can be used as the basis for designing products, for initiat-
ing a research programme, for supporting investment in a market sector—or,
most likely, as a starting point for more thinking. Table 13.3 gives a sample of
the output from a Delphi project undertaken some time ago which sought to
identify long-term trends.[7] It shows the future time-scale for the introduction of
new technologies.

Table 13.3    Long-term technology trends

| Item | Years 5 | 10 | 15 |
|---|---|---|---|
| A    Universal data bank | ———— | | |
|       New source of energy | | | |
| B    sea oil | | ———— | |
| C    solar | | | ———— |
| D    water/wind | | | ———— |
| E    Full sensory 'telephone' | ———— | | |
|       Cheap materials for publication purposes | | | |
| F    manual | | ——— | |
| G    automated | | ——— | |
| H    Cheap universal teaching machines and programmes for TV | ———————————————— | | |
| I    Cheap new food sources (sea-farming, etc | | ———————— | |
|       Thought transfer | | | |
| J    by indirect means | | | ———— |
| K    directly—brain to brain transfer | | | |
|       Artificial intelligence | | | |
| L    largely possible | | ——— | |
| M    completely possible | | ———— | |
| N    Cheap materials for building houses, ships, aircraft | | | ———— |

Despite the apparent simplicity of the Delphi method, it is difficult to undertake successfully. Firstly, the panel members have to be experts in the subject discussed; but they must also be able to communicate with one another and, in particular, none must be permitted to dominate the process. In general, the maverick solution is eliminated by the procedures and only the consensus view survives. It may be, however, that the maverick view was the only one worth listening to. It is rare that day-to-day marketing problems may be solved in this way, but if Plinmo wanted to know the extent to which large plastic mouldings might be adapted to new applications in the home within the next 10 years, it represents a usefully structured way of starting the investigation.

## Spreadsheets

A spreadsheet is an array of data contained on a computer; the data may be projected forward and manipulated in order to show how the picture will change over time. The most common use is to show how revisions to operating items will affect the financial results of a business. Thus, a number of variations in the cost structure may be tested through to trading profit, profit before tax (taking into account the consequent needs for more or less financing) and earnings. The balance sheet may be similarly modified.

The spreadsheet does nothing more than could be done with a quill pen and a wet towel by a competent accountant, but it does it at a speed that effectively removes any limit to the number of 'what if' questions which may be usefully posed and considered. A particular application for an organization such as Conglom is to test the implications of acquisitions and disposals. These transactions can be very complex and a quick reading of the impact on earnings per share, debt–equity ratio, profitability and cash flow enables the planner to take a view of the impact on key ratios. It gives guidance on whether any particular acquisition is possible at the sort of price that is likely to be acceptable, or what the minimum price on a disposal should be to provide a better future cash flow for the company.

There are a number of different spreadsheet packages available on microcomputers of which VisiCalc on a Hewlett Packard, or Lotus 1–2–3 on an IBM PC, are good examples. The method is that of computer programming and the output may be made to conform to whatever layout (within the constraints of the machine) that the operator desires.

### Regression analysis

A time trend, as in Fig. 8.4, is a technique that almost every manager has used at some time to illuminate some aspect of his business. This is the simplest form of regression. The experience curve shown in Fig. 13.5 was a slightly more complex example, where price was regressed against cumulative production.

Some particularly useful areas for time trends are:

- economic data
- sales and profits
- costs as a proportion of sales
- productivity indices
- working capital as a proportion of sales

By converting such data to graphical form, an immediate view on trend and current direction can be obtained. On the other hand, it is rarely very helpful to produce a time trend of capital expenditure or cash flow. Capital expenditure rarely shows any trend, except over a very extended period and the observations on any graph are heavily phased. It might usefully be shown as a proportion of depreciation over time, either to indicate the adequacy of the expenditure—or of the depreciation provision. Cash flow, however, incorporates so many influences that a simple regression is probably of little value.

At the other end of the scale of sophistication, regressions may be grouped together to build complete models of a business. In architectural terms, these have the structure of a Westminster Abbey compared with the wayside shrine of a simple time trend.[8] The use of such models is discussed particularly in Chapter 8. From the practical point of view, it has to be recognized that the specialists who build them have to apply a degree of experimentation. While the research has to be directed by some rational theory, the actual construction work can be very hit and miss. Thus, a model of the plastic sacks market might take just a few weeks to build, or it could run into months—or it might indeed never be achieved. This implies a relatively high cost. So, the use of this technique is something to embark upon only if the pay-off is going to be high in helping to manage the business.

## Cross-sectional analysis

This technique involves the assessment of the respective influences of a variety of factors upon some characteristic of the business. For example, it is worth considering the relative importance to return on investment of marketing, promotion, research, product quality and so on; what would be the best mixture among all of these management options, to maximize the profitability of a particular product? In cross-sectional analysis, this is done not by comparing these factors on a one-to-one basis, but by looking at them altogether as a package. Thus, the technique has obvious advantages over matrices as it can theoretically cope with any number of factors at a time. On the other hand, the output lacks the immediate appeal of a matrix as it normally comes out as a string of relationships which then have to be translated into some other form. This will, indeed, often be a matrix. Nevertheless, the method offers a much deeper and more comprehensive analysis of any business.

The leading exponent of this type of analysis is the Strategic Planning Institute of Cambridge, Mass.[9] Their research is based on a data base going back about 20 years which encompasses the history of over 2500 separate businesses. The PIMS programme measures businesses along a large number of dimensions that have been identified as having an impact upon profitability. They have demonstrated correlations between these factors and profitability, cash flow, productivity and other features of a business.

Using this system, Plinmo might wish to address the question of what its profit level ought to be, given its market, production and personnel stance. The exercise in Tables 13.4 and 13.5 shows how this is done. For reasons of brevity, it is not based upon the full PIMS model, but on the more limited LIM model. The principles remain the same. The inputs required and their responses from Plinmo's management are shown in the worked example in Table 13.4.

The print-out in response to this information is given in Table 13.5. The analysis shows that, despite a somewhat weak relative market share, the business gains substantially from its product quality. On the other hand, it has excessive investment intensity and productivity is low. Finally, it suffers from a

**Table 13.4**   The PIMS programme

This worksheet is an aid to gathering data for the PIMS Limited Information Model. For definition of terms, please refer to the accompanying text.

1. Calendar Year   19 **85**

Market Shares of:

2. This Business   **17.0** %
3. Largest competitor   **22.0** %
4. Second Largest Competitor   **18.0** %
5. Third Largest Competitor   **12.0** %
6. Three Largest Competitors (Lines 3+4+5)   **52.0** %
7. Relative Market Share (2÷6) × 100   **33.0** %
8. Industry Concentration (Share of 4 Largest Producers)   **69.0** %

Percentage of this Business' Sales from:

9. Superior products   **60** %
10. Equivalent Products   **40** %
11. Inferior Products   **–** %
12. Relative Product Quality (9–11)   **60** %
13. Relative Price (Price Parity with Competition = 100)   **110** %
14. New Products (Introduced in the Last Three Years) as a Percentage of Total Sales   **10** %
15. Number of Immediate Customers that Account for 50% of this Business' Sales   **200**
*16. Typical Purchase Amount by Immediate Customer (Use Index)   **5**

146

## INCOME STATEMENT

| | $000 | PERCENT OF SALES |
|---|---|---|
| 17. Net Sales | $ 3123 | 100 % |
| 18. Purchases | 1163 | 37.2 |
| 19. Value Added (17–18) | $ 1960 | 62.8 % |
| 20. Manufacturing and Distribution | 1344 | 43.0 |
| 21. Depreciation | 241 | 7.7 |
| 22. Total Marketing | 320 | 10.2 |
| 23. Total R & D | 95 | 3.0 |
| 24. Administrative and Other Expenses | 213 | 6.9 |
| 25. Pretax Income (*before* Interest charges) | $ 378 | 12.1 % |

## BALANCE SHEET
(Enter average for the year)

| | $000 | PERCENT OF SALES |
|---|---|---|
| 26. Receivables | 718 | 23.0 % |
| 27. Inventories | 598 | 19.1 |
| 28. Current Liabilities | 486 | 15.6 |
| 29. Working Capital (26+27−28) | $ 830 | 26.6 % |
| 30. Gross Plant & Equipment | 2354 | 75.3 |
| 31. Net Plant & Equipment | 1512 | 48.4 |
| 32. Other Assets | – | – |
| 33. Investment (29+31+32) | $ 2342 | 75.0 |

| | | |
|---|---|---|
| 34. Actual ROI (25+33) | 16.1 | % |
| 35. Number of Employees | 56 | |
| 36. Value Added per Employee (19+35 in $000 U.S.) | $ 58 | |
| 37. Percent of Total Employees Unionized | 45 | % |
| 38. Capacity Utilization | 74 | % |
| 39. *Real Growth of Served Market Over the Last 3–5 Years (Per Annum)* | 8 | % |

| *Index | Purchase Amount |
|---|---|
| 1 | $0–1 |
| 2 | $1–10 |
| 3 | $10–100 |
| 4 | $100–1,000 |
| 5 | $1,000–10,000 |
| 6 | $10,000–100,000 |
| 7 | $100,000–1 million |
| 8 | $1–10 million |
| 9 | Over $10 million |

© 1982, The Strategic Planning Institute

**Table 13.5**   Limited information model

ESTIMATE OF NORMAL ROI
BY CATEGORY OF IMPACT

| FACTORS | | PIMS MEAN | THE BUSINESS | IMPACT OF FACTOR ON ESTIMATE OF ROI (%) | |
|---|---|---|---|---|---|
| 1 Market share index | : | | | −2.0 | |
|    market share (%) | : | 23.4 | 17.0 | | |
|    relative market share (%) | : | 62.1 | 33.0 | | |
| 2 Relative product quality | : | 25.8 | 60.0 | 4.3 | |
| 3 Unionization (%) | : | 43.0 | 74.0 | 0.0 | |
| 4 New product sales/sales (%) | : | 10.3 | 10.0 | 1.9 | |
| 5 R & D expenditure/sales (%) | : | 2.2 | 3.0 | −0.1 | |
| 6 Marketing expenditure/sales (%) | : | 9.3 | 10.2 | −0.3 | |
| | Competitive position and action | | | | 3.9 |
| 7 Investment intensity index | : | | | | |
|    Investment/sales (%) | : | 52.8 | 75.0 | −2.9 | |
|    Investment/value added (%) | : | 96.0 | 119.4 | | |
| 8 Value added/sales (%) | : | 56.0 | 62.8 | | |
| 9 Labour productivity | : | 100.0 | 72.2 | 0.4 | |
| 10 GBV of P & E/investment (%) | : | 89.1 | 100.8 | −5.3 | |
|    GBV of P & E/sales (%) | : | 46.5 | 75.7 | −0.6 | |
| 11 Receivables/investment (%) | : | 32.7 | 30.7 | | |
|    Receivables/sales (%) | : | 15.1 | 23.0 | −0.2 | |
| 12 Capacity utilization (%) | : | 75.6 | 74.0 | | |
| | | | | −0.5 | |
| | Capital and production structure | | | | −9.1 |
| 13 Real market growth rate (% p.a.) | : | 4.2 | 8.0 | 0.2 | |
| 14 Industry concentration (%) | : | 57.5 | 69.0 | 0.6 | |
| 15 Number of immed. custmrs. = 50% sls | : | 337.2 | 200.0 | −1.0 | |
| 16 Purchase amount immediate custmrs. | : | 5.3 | 5.0 | 0.6 | |
| | Environment and customer features | | | | 0.4 |

TOTAL IMPACT     −4.8
AVERAGE ROI, ALL PIMS BUSINESSES     21.5

ESTIMATED ROI, THIS BUSINESS     16.7
DEVIATION FROM ESTIMATED ROI, THIS BUSINESS     −0.6

ACTUAL ROI, THIS BUSINESS     16.1

fragmented customer base. All these problems appear to be capable of treatment by the right sort of management action and it can be seen where the biggest pay-offs in changed tactics might be.

## Expert systems

In concluding this discussion of techniques, some mention should be made of the potential benefit of expert systems.[10] This is the name given to the engineering of the knowledge of an expert into a computer system which may then be used by others to gain access to that knowledge in a routine way. Thus, medical expert systems capture the ability of a leading authority in a particular area— e.g., a specialist in the treatment of microbial infections—to diagnose and prescribe the best drugs. The system sets up interrogation routines on symptoms which, correctly answered by the operator, enable the machine to indicate the most likely diagnoses and the most appropriate treatments. It provides explanations to the operator who is enabled to tap into the skill of the expert.

These systems are being increasingly developed in medicine, geology, metallurgy and similar sciences. Some start has been made on tax and finance.[11] The problems of planning are somewhat more difficult to tackle in this context, because there are no acknowledged experts who are competent both in all the planning skills and in managing all types of business. It is almost like trying to develop a single methodology for the diagnosis of all disease. As a result, no expert system has been adequately developed in this area, as yet. Nevertheless, there are possibilities of producing something useful and work has started. The interrogation procedures will probably take the form of a series of checklists for managers to run through and the outputs will then consist of suggested strategic and tactical options, of the sort discussed in Part 1. This would be available on floppy disc for use on a PC.

## Conclusion

Only a small number of particular techniques have been tackled in the foregoing discussion and only a flavour of these has been given. What is important to recognize is that different problems require different approaches. Sometimes a simple matrix will do; at other times, it becomes important to undertake an analysis of the business in depth. Planners must have available the full range of methods and in advising their chief executive, they should certainly not be wedded to any single one.

## Notes

1. W. J. Chandler and P. H. W. Cockle, *Techniques of Scenario Planning*, McGraw-Hill, Maidenhead, Berks, 1982, p. 29.

2. S. J. Q. Robinson *et al.*, 'The directional policy matrix—tool for strategic planning', *Long Range Planning* vol. II, no. 3, June 1978, pp. 8–15.
3. B. Taylor, 'Managing the process of corporate development', *The Realities of Planning*, Pergamon Press, Oxford, 1982, pp. 115–118.
4. Source internal to Reed International PLC, based on industry statistics.
5. R. V. L. Wright, *Strategic Centers—A Contemporary Managing System*, Arthur D. Little, Cambridge, Mass., 1975, p. 9.
6. For a comprehensive survey, see for example W. L. Brockhaus and J. F. Mickelson, 'An analysis of prior Delphi applications and some observations on its future applicability', *Technological Forecasting and Social Change* no. 10, Elsevier North Holland, New York, 1977, pp. 103–110.
7. F. H. George, *Problem Solving*, Duckworth, London, 1980, pp. 183 *et seq.*
8. *Techniques of Scenario Planning, op. cit.*, p. 57. For regression techniques, see Appendix 4, p. 149, *et seq.*
9. S. Schoeffler, 'Nine basic findings on business strategy', *Pimsletter on Business Strategy* no. 1, Strategic Planning Institute, Cambridge, Mass., 1977.
10. A useful survey is given in L. Johnson and E. T. Kernavou, *Expert Systems Technology—A Guide*, Abacus Press, London, 1985.
11. *Expert Systems for the Finance Industry*, Papers presented to a Management Seminar, London, July 1982, sponsored jointly by SPL International and Intelligent Terminals Ltd. of Oxford.

# 14

# Plan procedures

## Structuring the planning round

The planning process cascades down from objectives to strategies and thence to tactics and financing. Any hydraulic analogy, however, fails at this point, because water will not flow uphill, and one of the necessary features of planning is feedback. Furthermore, a clear distinction is not normally made between strategies and tactics (as described earlier) when actually preparing plans.

In setting up procedures, therefore, the emphasis is not on the objectives–strategies–tactics classification, but rather on the time-scale within which actions are expected to be effected and effective. The relevant periods are:

- long range—a period of the order of three years and beyond
- annual—as the name suggests, what will happen next year
- monthly—phasing of plans has to be undertaken for control purposes

Few businesses are prepared to devote time to three separate planning rounds in a year. Too much thinking and not enough doing is the complaint. Whatever the merits of this view, an excessive amount of time devoted to preparation of documents and reconciling figures is not advocated.

## Alternative approaches—a plan and a budget

There are a number of different approaches of which two are described. The first rolls up the long-range and annual plans into one. Strategic changes in the form of alternative long-term goals are discussed and then the specific actions that flow from this are nominated in the form of annual targets. The figures will include projections for three, four or five years forward, of which the first year is, at this stage, only indicative. The next stage is the preparation of a fully phased budget, on a month-by-month basis, of the first year's plan, as approved. The manager is then committed to these figures.

The advantages of this system are as follows:

- It avoids the need for prolonged statements on strategies every year—broadly once they have been set and are working, they do not need frequent reconsideration.

- It concentrates the exploration of options to one period in the planning process; there is no time lag between agreeing strategies and setting tactics.
- Once the overall plans are agreed, the manager has then a firm basis on which to work out the figures.
- Provided these budget figures conform to the agreed plan, there is no need for any further review.

Its disadvantages are:

- The amalgamation of the long- and short-range plans almost always results in emphasis on the short-term. The longer-term numbers are often little more than a handle cranking exercise.
- Even if adequate time is devoted to the longer term, the inclusion of an annual plan with specific proposals tends to pre-empt the adoption of alternative options—all the pressures are against working the annual plan through again and the system tends to take strategic direction out of the hands of the chief executive.

## A long-range and a short-term plan

An alternative is the separation of the process into a long-range and a short-term plan. It is not necessary for *all* the strategies to be discussed every year. This should be done, say, every three years. In the intervening period only the critical long-term problems are addressed. The short-term plan includes projections for only one year and it is prepared in accordance with the strategic guidelines resulting from the long-range plan discussions. The phasing is carried out as part of the short-term plan, but may be treated as a routine exercise, to be undertaken after the plans have been approved.

The following are the advantages of such a system:

- It provides an adequate and separate opportunity for consideration of long-term aspects affecting the business, unpressurized by short-term problems; the quality of the figures and judgements should be better.
- It allows greater freedom in the way in which strategic problems are tackled. Rather than having a formal document and being constrained by the formats and procedures of planning reviews, chief executives may prefer to sit down with a few of their aides and brainstorm; or they may prefer a chat over a few drinks with the manager concerned. Only in the full scale review, conducted every three years, do they have to go through all the planning formalities.
- It enables top management to provide strategic guidelines within which the short-term plans are to be prepared—the opportunities for managers to pre-empt the chief executive are more limited.

On the other hand, the system has some disadvantages:

- Two sets of figures are required, at least every three years, the first for the long-range and the second for the short-term. This could degenerate into a reconciliation exercise where the planner's main task is to 'hunt the discrepancy'.
- Generally speaking, two sets of meetings are required, though not with all the business managers.
- The gap between settling long-term direction for the businesses and short-term action means that the planning for the latter may be held up where any particular strategy is under review.

## The need for flexibility

The choice of approach depends on the management style of the chief executive. Whichever it is, it has to be used flexibly so that the process does not get bogged down in unnecessary detail or, in the case of a group, grind to a halt through lack of a component plan. In a small business, a man like Jack Robinson could postpone any part of the programme to enable him to deal with a more urgent problem.

This is more difficult in a large organization where the decision-making process is more bureaucratic, and the consolidation of the plan can only proceed at the pace of the slowest business. Furthermore, if Sir James Forbes and his board have just decided to sell division 'A' and buy a new major business 'B', this has the potential to cause chaos to the standard planning procedures. Conglom would have to adopt in its annual business plan provisions for costs of acquisition and disposal, estimates of realizations on sales and less than familiar forecasts for the new activities which would certainly not have been produced in Conglom's formats. These have to be put together to provide an adequate set of figures for the forthcoming year, not least to enable the business to be financed properly.

## The planning calendar

The realities of the commercial world demand a formal timetable. An example, based upon the second alternative outlined above of separate long-range and annual plans, is given in Table 14.1. It is assumed that the company concerned adopts the national fiscal year, and that its year ends on 31 March or thereabouts. It is also assumed that this is the occasion for a full-scale long-term review.

The planning year starts with a post mortem on the previous year. This will involve all the staff who were involved in administering the programme at the individual business level as well as centrally. This then develops naturally into the formulation of the next instructions for the long-range plan, and probably notes for the short-term instructions to be produced later in the year. This post

**Table 14.1**    Planning calendar

| Date | Action |
| --- | --- |
| May | Review previous year's procedures |
| June | Prepare and issue instructions for long-range plan |
| July | Prepare individual long-range plans by SBU |
| | Produce long-term base-case assumptions and economic review |
| August | Produce alternative scenarios |
| | Consider central issues for debate |
| September | Submit SBU long-range plans |
| | Analyse plan submissions |
| October | Review SBU long-range plans |
| | Prepare overall long-range plan/financing |
| November | Approve overall long-range plan |
| | Amend last year's estimates in previous year's plan |
| | Undertake half year review of current SBU plans |
| | Update base-case scenario |
| | Prepare and issue guidelines, assumptions and instructions for short-term plan |
| December | Produce short-term plans by SBU and for central departments |
| January | Submit SBU short-term plans |
| | Analyse SBU short-term plans |
| | Reforecast scenarios |
| February | Review SBU short-term plans |
| | Prepare overall short-term plan |
| March | Approve overall short-term plan |
| | Authorize individual short-term plan |
| | Phase SBU short-term plans |

mortem is a useful sounding board, but whoever chairs the session must be reasonably tough to avoid trying to please everyone. Individual businesses will always complain that the timing is wrong for them, that the information is inappropriate and that the centre takes too long or demands too much. In the end, what the chief executive wants is what must happen; if the others can all be accommodated, so much the better—though during the discussion they can all be allowed to let off steam.

## Timing

The time allowed for the various items in the calendar will vary with the complexity of the organization. It is vital, however, to ensure that those who have to make judgements have enough reading and thinking time. Sir James Forbes with his four major divisions should have at least three days per division to read and absorb the information. This means twelve working days and in practice a maximum of something like three weeks between submission and review. The review will take another week and then the staff will assemble a draft of the overall plan. Again, there has to be time to think about this, not just in the context of the reviews but also against alternative economic futures and in the light of alternative strategic opportunities not dealt with in individual business plans.

Where there are major strategic changes, it is possible that the plan timetable will overrun, but it is better that it should do so than that incomplete, or inadequately considered plans are adopted. If it means that the chief executive cannot finally authorize the guidelines for the short-term plan of any SBU in time, the procedures should continue but on the understanding that the short-term plan may have to be revised at a later date.

Finally, in the context of timing, it should be a golden rule that only the chief executive is permitted to change the timing of the planning round. This will obviously be the case in the small business, but in larger ones there is constant pressure for more time. Nevertheless, the problem of trying to consolidate plan figures and to deal coherently with a multiplicity of different businesses is made impossible if the businesses do not send their plans in on time or if they have freedom to change the dates of the meetings.

## Review meetings

An important feature of the planning process is the meeting face to face of those who have prepared the plans and those responsible for approving (or rejecting) them. There is no set rule as to who should attend such meetings except that, like all such assemblies, they tend to be effective in inverse proportion to the numbers present, so that one to one gets most done. However, such meetings can have a use in getting a particular executive to plead some special case or in exposing him to the higher echelons of management. Further, the manager of the business may want expert assistance or flank protection.

A frequent practice at such meetings is that of making a presentation. Unless there is some specific topic not covered by the plan on which further information is sought, the chief executive should fight off any such move. Generally speaking, a presentation is made (literally) in the dark, using slides that are often not reconciled with the plan. This makes it difficult to challenge the material. It normally provides a reinforcement only of what is said in the plan and is, therefore, not necessary. It postpones getting down to the real issues, perhaps until time runs out.

In conducting a review, it is not necessary to go through every aspect of the plan. There is a tendency to let each manager have a say, but again, this is time-consuming; if individual speakers are performing well and in line with expectations, their bonus should be that they will not be called upon to justify anything other than exceptional items.

The various techniques for analysis of plans are discussed in the next chapter. The review meeting must never be allowed to degenerate into a mere nit-picking exercise, with smart accountants or planners pointing out discrepancies in the details of the plan submissions. If it does seem that there is likely to be a lot of detail to go over, there should be a staff meeting to iron out the minutiae before the main discussion. Furthermore, if analysis of the proposals indicates any major problems, the managers concerned should be advised in advance. The review procedure and planning generally will become quickly discredited if it appears to be only a numbers game, or an opportunity to score points.

## Approval of plans

Where, following review, a plan is approved, it is important that the manager concerned should be informed, whether by the chief executive signing a copy of the plan as approved, or by writing formally to that effect. Often a plan is approved only conditionally, e.g. subject to the agreement of a specific level of capital expenditure and, again, any such condition must be unequivocally indicated.

Where, however, some major aspect of a plan is to be changed, this makes it impossible to give it the seal of approval, even conditionally. In such an event, the manager concerned will be required to rework it. This may put out the whole planning timetable. If the business affected is one of a number in a group, the best way to deal with the situation, in order to avoid holding up the rest of the organization, is to include the details of the plan in the consolidation but modified by a central provision to take account of the anticipated change. When a new, acceptable plan is submitted, this may be substituted, though there may still be some small provision to cover the difference between the finally approved document and what was originally included for this particular business.

It may be that the chief executive is uneasy about a plan, but does not want to change the numbers. In this situation, the plan should be approved with the concerns indicated. At the same time, it may be considered prudent to make some central provisions against the optimism (or pessimism) of the business manager involved. Examples of an approach to provisions are included in Chapter 15.

## Aids to implementation

Implementing a plan is a whole book in its own right. It is the responsibility of operating management. Nevertheless, the implementation can be assisted by the way in which the organization approaches its planning. There are four key factors:

- Overt dedication to the process by chief executives; unless they make it clear that they treat planning seriously and that it is one of the primary mechanisms through which they intend to run their business, there will be little enthusiasm among their managers for it.

- Direct access by chief executives to the SBU; if chief executives are insulated from the businesses where independent strategic decisions are being made, they will not get first hand information and control is weakened. Obviously, in a very large organization they must delegate some of this responsibility, but they should never be denied and, indeed, should take the opportunity to talk directly to the manager of a SBU where it is useful for them to do so. If they do not do this, their position approximates to that of banker rather than manager.

- Involve management in the planning process to as high a level as possible; if strategies cannot be accepted or plans are changed for reasons of overall policy, even though they may be appropriate at the SBU level, it is important to ensure that the reasons are understood by the managers, even if they are not entirely accepted. The principle also means that, so far as may be, managers should be encouraged to follow their own preferred strategies. In the absence of very compelling reasons, it is better to back an effective manager than to impose an unwelcome direction on his or her plans.

In conclusion, an effective way of achieving the most lively interest of managers in the planning process is by linking it to their rewards for success or sanctions for failure. Many businesses still measure reward according to last year's profit or cash flow. If planning is really to take root, however, reward should be linked to the strategic goals and tactical targets agreed for any business—and a high overshoot of a soft target is as bad (though not so painful) as an undershoot of a reasonable one. Such an approach would guarantee to planning both an adequate degree of application by all executives concerned and a strong sense of realism in taking on commitments for the business in the future.

# 15

# Reviewing plans

All the techniques discussed in Chapter 13 may have been usefully deployed in preparing the plans. In analysing them for review, however, a somewhat simpler approach is adopted, namely good, old-fashioned eyeballing. The chief executive and the management team look at the proposals and where they do not understand or have doubts, they ask questions. To enable them to do this more easily, they will take advantage of simple time series. Experienced managers will be able to get an adequate feel for some of the figures just by reading them, but even for them, the translation of data into graphical form gives a very quick fix on both long-term trends and the direction of the latest movements.

Table 15.1 gives the figures for Industrial Services Limited (IS), one of Conglom's divisions. Converted into a graph, the data appear as in Fig. 15.1. At a glance, it can be seen that:

- the strategy is to milk the market, taking more in price than in volume;
- the pricing tactics are adventurous, expecting a faster rate of increase than has been sustained historically, even though inflation at the time is slowing; an experience curve might be useful;
- the volumes, though not rising quite as fast in the first year of the plan as in the previous two years, are not perceived to be affected by the pricing policy, as they were in 1977;
- the trade cycle seems to have been ignored. Conglom's CEO was well aware that 1976 was a recovery year from his experience of the previous cyclical downturn which had, of course, been exacerbated by the oil price crisis. He

Table 15.1  Industrial services and price volumes

|  | Actual | | | | Est | Plan | | |
|---|---|---|---|---|---|---|---|---|
|  | 1975 | 1976 | 1977 | 1978 | 1979 | 1980 | 1981 | 1982 |
| Volume index | 75 | 85 | 84 | 90 | 96 | 100 | 104 | 108 |
| Price index | 62 | 68 | 73 | 76 | 87 | 100 | 109 | 117 |

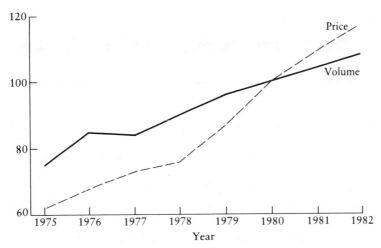

**Figure 15.1**   Industrial Services sales

would be concerned to know when the next downturn would be likely to occur and how severe it would be.

In the event, the division's forecasts were hit for six by the next oil price crisis and the cyclical recession which came in right on cue in 1980. Growth after that has been slow and margins have been depressed. This highlights the need for an informed view of the economy and the individual markets at the time the plans are reviewed.

### Setting the scene

To illustrate the process, therefore, a review by Conglom of its operating plans is simulated, starting with the base-case economic forecast.[1] This was as in Table 15.2, at the macroeconomic level.

The forecast figures were the assumptions underlying the various more detailed forecasts for the individual markets for IS. Alternative scenarios were prepared, including another oil price crisis, as mentioned in Chapter 8. This last gave an alternative set of assumptions which were treated as the worst case

**Table 15.2**   Base-case economic forecast

| % change | 1980 | 1981 | 1982 | 1983 |
|----------|------|------|------|------|
| GDP | − 0.5 | 1.9 | 4.0 | 5.3 |
| WPI | 10.3 | 10.3 | 9.4 | 8.3 |

**Table 15.3**    Worst case scenario

| % change | 1980 | 1981 | 1982 | 1983 |
|----------|------|------|------|------|
| GDP | −3.4 | −2.8 | 3.0 | 6.8 |
| WPI | 12.5 | 15.0 | 9.4 | 5.1 |

within which the business would make plans (see Table 15.3). The base-case was treated as the best case.

The substantial recovery in 1983 demonstrated by the figures in Table 15.3 represented a bounce-back by the UK economy in a high oil price regime, but without any further adverse changes such as excessive wage inflation and industrial unrest. It was accompanied by a high pound and a high consequent level of imports. This was a reasonably probable scenario to try in 1979. In retrospect, it did capture some of the actual events in the short term, though it substantially underestimated the actual oil price increase that occurred.[2] In the following review, Conglom makes provision in its plans against this worst case.

## Conglom's sales

Conglom's four divisional plans are given in Appendix 1 and the following commentaries are based on them. IS's sales were considered above; its price (*P*) and volume (*V*) indices based on 1975 are reproduced in Fig. 15.2 with those of the other three divisions.

The other three divisions' strategies and tactics, as revealed in these graphs, are as follows:

- Consumer Services (CS)
  - a strategy of milking the market strongly
  - prices are pushed up fast, but volumes are allowed to fall back as a result (a reasonably credible picture)
  - no allowance for cyclicality
- Consumer Manufacturers (CM)
  - changing from a strategy of increasing market share to one of modest milking
  - prices move up at a relatively limited pace
  - again no allowance for cyclicality
- Industrial Manufacturers (IM)
  - no real strategy but a reaction to market forces
  - volumes recovered from the last recession, but since then have fallen again, while prices move in a straight line (oblivious of tactical options)
  - perhaps some indication of cyclicality (fortuitous?)

## Cost analysis

Figure 15.3 shows costs as a percentage of sales for IS. This is more useful than

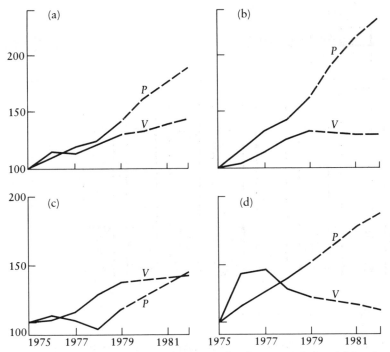

**Figure 15.2**  Conglom divisional prices and volumes. (a) Industrial Services; (b) Consumer Services; (c) Consumer Manufacturers; (d) Industrial Manufacturers.

looking at the absolute amounts, as they are bound to vary with the level of activity.

The best comparisons for these items of cost could, in fact, be different for each of the components; for example:

- raw materials and energy      – as percentage of output (sales plus change in inventories)
- direct employment      – as percentage of value added
- other employment and 'other' costs      – as percentage of total costs

Nevertheless, to enable the data to be contained in one diagram, sales are used as the criterion. It provides, in any event, the added satisfaction that the percentages should add up to 100 (roundings permitting), if profit margin is included.

The picture presented is undeniably one of a profitable business with good margins. These have improved principally as a result of the steady decline in raw material costs as a proportion of sales. The manager of this division is adopting a cautious approach in assuming no change in this ratio for the future. Ignoring the unknowable (by how much oil prices would go up and affect

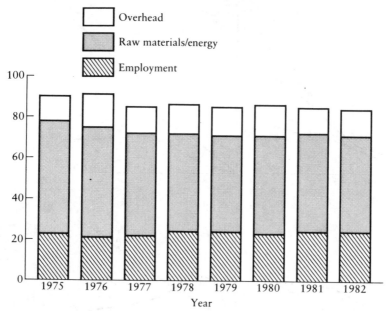

**Figure 15.3**    Industrial Services cost analysis

prices and demand), he should, nevertheless, have foreseen that 1980 was likely to suffer a cyclical downturn. Would this mean higher or lower costs? What was the experience in the previous recession? These were the sorts of questions Conglom would be asking him.

As a check, an experience curve could be drawn for the raw materials market as a whole, but this would only show long-term trends. An extrapolation of the actuals for the last five years gives the picture in Fig. 15.4. The trend line suggests that there is more improvement to go for, but the cycle is flattening out. In view of the uncertainties surrounding 1980, the attitude adopted by management in its plan seems sensible.

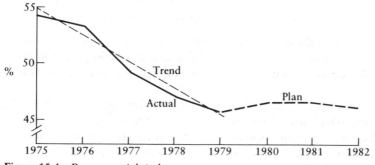

**Figure 15.4**    Raw materials/sales percentage

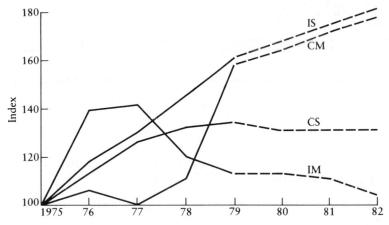

**Figure 15.5**    Productivity indices (1975 = 100)

**Table 15.4**    Industrial Services employees

|  | Actual | | | | Est | Plan | | |
|---|---|---|---|---|---|---|---|---|
|  | 1975 | 1976 | 1977 | 1978 | 1979 | 1980 | 1981 | 1982 |
| Number of employees | 760 | 686 | 671 | 671 | 671 | 657 | 657 | 660 |

## Employment costs

There is increased investment in plant and equipment (note the doubling in depreciation as a proportion of sales). It seems disappointing, therefore, that employment costs have recently increased by up to 2 per cent of sales, allowing that 1976 may have been an exceptional year. Is it not possible to get back to the opening ratio or even better? This could be an area in which to apply pressure. In particular, if the sales forecasts are over-optimistic with their 20 per cent increase in 1980, what room will there be to pull back on employment costs if they fail to hit the turnover target?

This leads to a closer look at this cost sector. First, it becomes clear that improved productivity in terms of output has been a preoccupation of the management. The graph in Fig. 15.5 shows that IS has been Conglom's star performer up to 1979 in this respect, and was promising more. The criterion used was output *per capita*. The number of employees in IS was certainly reducing (see Table 15.4) and output was increasing.

So why were employment costs rising? It turned out that the average remuneration per head had gone up very steeply (see Table 15.5). Remuneration includes pensions payments and 1978 was a special year, as improved benefits

**Table 15.5**   Industrial Services remuneration

| | Actual | | | | Est | Plan | | |
|---|---|---|---|---|---|---|---|---|
| | 1975 | 1976 | 1977 | 1978 | 1979 | 1980 | 1981 | 1982 |
| Average remuneration per head | 3570 | 4185 | 4860 | 6110 | 7150 | 8435 | 9740 | 10775 |
| % change per annum | | 17.2 | 16.1 | 25.7 | 17.0 | 18.0 | 15.5 | 10.6 |

were introduced. Nevertheless, the increases were still very large and in excess of inflation. Two questions arose:

1 Was the improved productivity bought at too high a price in wages and social costs?
2 Would it be feasible to keep down to the relatively low 10.6 per cent increase in 1982 (upon which margins for that year were necessarily dependent)?

These and many other questions arise out of the data provided on costs.

### Working capital
Moving ahead to the balance sheet, IS does not have a high working capital-to-sales ratio, so the example of Industrial Manufacturers (IM) which makes trucks, is used to illustrate this part of the review. The recovery in truck sales in 1976 was not matched by an equivalent increase in inventories until 1977, by which time demand was beginning to slacken and all the competition was also producing at higher levels of capacity utilization.

The graph in Fig. 15.6 demonstrates how capacity utilization apparently mir-

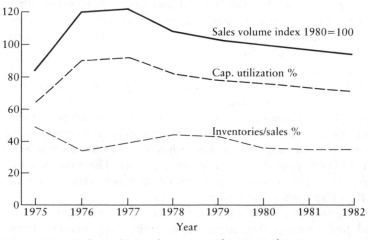

**Figure 15.6**   Industrial Manufacturers working capital

**Table 15.6**   Industrial Manufacturing debtors/creditors

|  | Actual | | | | Est | Plan | | |
|---|---|---|---|---|---|---|---|---|
|  | 1975 | 1976 | 1977 | 1978 | 1979 | 1980 | 1981 | 1982 |
| Debtors less creditors £m | 1.3 | 2.4 | 2.5 | 2.5 | 2.6 | 1.2 | 1.4 | 1.5 |
| % of sales | 9.1 | 10.2 | 9.5 | 9.8 | 9.8 | 4.2 | 4.6 | 4.8 |

rored demand, as indicated by sales volumes. The inventory to sales line, however, shows that production appears to have been caught short by the 1976 resurgence in demand. After that the plant over-produced. It seems to have been the fault of market intelligence rather than production management, as the latter did appear to have been able to adjust reasonably fast. This is typical of a production oriented business.

Another interesting feature to investigate is the debtor–creditor balance (see Table 15.6). It appears that the business had been financing itself through its creditors to the extent of 10 per cent of sales. An interesting comparison is the level of this ratio for British Leyland (see Chapter 10). For what reason is it planned to cut this source of finance in half? Is it forced upon the business by the pressure of competitors' practices, or is it to achieve some other advantage? Could it be the whim of some purchasing officer who is being pressurized by his suppliers?

In general, in view of the high levels of working capital involved and the lack of confidence that the figures generate, it might be worth while to undertake a PAR analysis of working capital, using the PIMS programme. The object is to try to answer the question 'what should the level of working capital be?'

This programme has analysed the experience of a large number of businesses and has found that working capital tends to rise:

- with rising sales force expenditure as a proportion of sales;
- as the importance of auxiliary services to end-users increases;
- less markedly, where the business has a higher proportion of products that are inferior to those of the competition;
- where a higher volume of sales are exported (though this effect tends to be strongly demonstrated only in the range of exports up to 12 per cent of industry sales);
- according to location of served market: the national North American market demands a higher level of working capital than does a region of the USA or of Europe;
- where purchases are made less frequently by end-users: less working capital is employed for businesses whose customers buy the product weekly rather than at longer intervals;

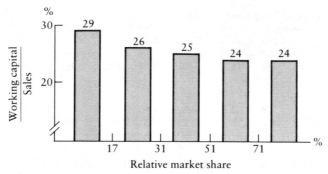

**Figure 15.7**    Working capital/market share

- the lower the capacity utilization;
- inversely with relative market share.

The bar chart in Fig. 15.7 exemplifies the last of such relationships and indicates how working capital as a percentage of sales is higher for those businesses with low relative market shares and vice versa.

By utilizing this sort of analysis, it may be possible to adapt the thrust of the business, for example by focusing on customers who will order ahead, by pruning the product line and by rationalizing suppliers.


### Fixed assets

The past and projected performance in the area of fixed assets is the next topic for review. Again, IM's record does not look very impressive. Understandably, capital expenditure has been restrained and in 1975 and 1976 it was only 50–60 per cent of replacement cost as capacity was allowed to run down in the depressed market environment. At the first hint of recovery, however, the engineers moved in and in 1977, 20 per cent more than replacement requirements was spent. It was cut back again as demand subsided and the events of 1976 were seen as a false dawn. So, it was the reading of the market place, rather than control of production which appears to have been at fault. The management's forecasts need very careful scrutiny, therefore, and perhaps projects for mothballing and even destruction of some equipment could be on the cards. The route that must be avoided lies in giving in to any pressure by the finance director to sell the plant cheaply to a competitor!

Compare this with IS's performance and plans, as shown in Table 15.7. The past gives much more confidence that expenditure is driven by realized expectations of demand. It may even be that there is excessive caution in laying out new plant. Nevertheless, this is a better fault in the market involved, which is mature and orderly, than being too far ahead in spending.

**Table 15.7**    Industrial Services sales, capacity and expenditure

|  | 1975 | 1976 | 1977 | 1978 | 1979 | 1980 | 1981 | 1982 |
|---|---|---|---|---|---|---|---|---|
| Sales volume index | 75 | 85 | 84 | 90 | 96 | 100 | 104 | 108 |
| Capacity utilization % | 76 | 83 | 86 | 94 | 100 | 102 | 97 | 95 |
| Capex/replacement depreciation % | 50 | 50 | 100 | 133 | 120 | 144 | 109 | 108 |

## Making plan provisions

Conglom will go through similar reviews for each of its divisions and the major constituent businesses. The same sort of questions will be asked by entrepreneurs looking at the plans for their own more limited span of activities, the only difference being that the larger group may adopt a more systematic approach, because of the lack of immediate personal experience among the corporate staff: it is easy to get out of touch after only a relatively short time away from the operations side of the business.

Having completed their reviews, both Sir James Forbes and Jack Robinson will want to make adjustments to the plans prepared by their managers. Based on the details in Appendix 1 and the foregoing commentaries, including the worst case scenario, Conglom might prepare some schedules as in Table 15.8. The provisions made are limited to the first plan year, but in practice, this exercise may be undertaken for each subsequent year.

The effect of the provisions is summarized below:

| Item | Plan £m | Provision £m | Result £m |
|---|---|---|---|
| Sales | 75.7 | (4.7) | 71.0 |
| Trading profit | 7.1 | (3.3) | 3.8 |
| Trading cash flow | 3.1 | (0.2) | 2.9 |

Note that of these provisions, the scenario accounts for £(2.1)m at the profit level and £(1.1)m at the cash flow level.

In making these provisions, one further decision is important: whether to impose them on the division or SBU, or to hold them centrally. The general rule is to pass out to the individual business or division the uncomfortable ones where they give rise to more testing targets, e.g., the lower working capital ratios, but to hold at the centre provisions against what may be considered to be optimistic targets. In this way, the managers are not presented with an early alibi for failure to hit the targets that they themselves have proposed. The provisions suggested by the scenarios should also be held centrally.

In conclusion, whether these provisions are worked out through a sophisticated programme or on the back of an envelope, they represent a realistic way of looking at what could happen to the business. Jobbing back, 1980 did turn

**Table 15.8**   Conglom plan provision

| Item | Business | Provision | Effect (£m) |
|---|---|---|---|
| Sales | IS | Abate price increases by 10% | (2.5) |
| | CS | Abate price increases by 10% | (0.9) |
| | Conglom | Reduce volumes to worst case scenario | (3.9) |
| | | Increase prices per worst case | 2.6 |
| Profit | IS | Hold margin at 1979 level, but on reduced sales | (0.4) |
| | CS | Reduced sales (no profit impact) | — |
| | CM | Slower recovery; no profit | (0.3) |
| | IM | Hold margin at 1979 ($-1.9\%$) | (0.5) |
| | Conglom | Worst case effect on sales | (0.1) |
| | | Worst case effect on cost structure | (2.0) |
| Working Capital | IS | Reduce to 17.5% on revised sales | 0.6 |
| | CM | Reduce by 2% of sales | 0.2 |
| | IM | Hold inventories, reduce debtor/creditor balance | 1.1 |
| | Conglom | Worst case effect on sales | (0.2) |
| | | Worst case effect on working capital ratio | 1.2 |
| Capex | IS | Accelerate programme | (0.1) |
| | CS | Reduce car/computer purchases | 0.2 |
| | IM | Reduce programme to minimum maintenance | 0.1 |

out to be a difficult year. Had Conglom pursued a proper review of its plans and made an assessment of possible adverse events and the effect these could have had, particularly on its cash flow, it would have been more ready to meet the crisis than many of its competitors.

## Notes

1. The base-case was substantially the forecast of Economic Models Ltd (now part of Data Resources Inc) prepared in mid-1979. For further details see W. J. Chandler and P. H. W. Cockle, *Techniques of Scenario Planning*, McGraw-Hill, Maidenhead, Berks., 1982, p. 105.
2. Finsbury Data Services, London, a real-time information bureau, quotes the *Financial Times*, *Guardian*, *Daily Telegraph* and *The Times* of 22 May 1980 on this issue, stating: 'the average posted price of OPEC oil is now $31.50 per barrel, compared to $25.50 last December (1979) and around $13 in January 1979'. We are now more or less back to January 1979 conditions.

# 16

# Control

## What control should cover

Imagine a scientist who has set up a most important experiment, upon whose success or failure large sums of money and even the welfare of sections of the community ultimately depend. This scientist's failure to monitor meticulously the results of such experiments at every level of significance would be rightly criticized as incompetent, displaying a disgraceful lack of concern for valuable resource and human lives. Yet, business people regularly 'experiment' with the individuals and money involved in their businesses without adequate checks on what is really going on. Certainly, most will review monthly sales and profit and cash flow, but how many are concerned to show how good a performance this represents in the various market places with which the business is involved? Even in an annual review, how many businesses check back to see what market share was proposed as a target and whether it was achieved? All the concentration is on the outward appearance of short-term health, as indicated by the accounting figures.

This concentration upon the short-term ability to generate profits and cash is an unfortunate characteristic of the UK business culture. As long ago as 1882 a Royal Commission[1] was to say:

> The Englishman is accustomed to seek for an immediate return and has yet to learn that an extended and systematic education, up to and including the methods of original research, is now a necessary preliminary to the fullest development of industry.

Not a lot has changed since then, as Elizabethan and Jacobean merchant adventurers remain our commercial heroes.

A small step in the right direction is the introduction of controls devoted to strategic goals as well as tactical targets, though the latter must not be neglected. In this way, plans that concentrate on markets and the long term will become meaningful rather than remaining an interesting exercise that has no practical significance. It has to be emphasized that planning without control is an empty endeavour.

It could be argued that having gone through the whole planning process, the targets such as those referred to in Chapter 7 are sufficient, that the strategies are automatically fulfilled by the achievement of these targets. This makes the assumption that, having prepared a plan, the rest of the world stands still.

Perhaps a market will grow faster or more slowly than expected, or suppliers will increase or reduce capacity more quickly than assumed, or exchange rates and interest rates will vary substantially from the base-case. All these events are possible, even likely. All critical factors, therefore, should be carefully monitored.

A second objection to this approach is the cost of all this analysis. How could a small business afford it? The answer must be that if the factor is important in planning, it has to be important to control and so the business *has* to afford it. However, the cost of maintaining awareness is not high. Chapter 12 discussed the various information sources and it would be unreal to suggest that the manager only goes out to gather information once a year. It is a continuous process. By structuring it and getting into the habit of marking down the key data, this will assist materially in focusing upon the critical.

Table 16.1 sets out some suggestions for non-accounting data which may be material to the plan. It relates to what the rest of the world is doing and emphasizes the need to maintain competitive advantage. In this table, the SBU is the unit being reviewed; A and B refer to the two major competitors in the market of product 'P'. The period chosen for producing the information may be whatever is appropriate (and possible).

The targets to be shown on the form will be those planned for the business concerned and the assumptions will be what was expected for the competition (or, in the case of finance, what was forecast for the market generally). Many spaces will be left blank, certainly, when such a system is first implemented, but gradually it will become easier to fill, as information gathering becomes more directed. Informed estimates will always be helpful where actuals are not known.

### Financial data

The above information basically acts as an explanation of the financial data. The financials, however, remain an essential element of reporting and control. Typical headings for a monthly report of the accounting figures are as shown in Fig. 16.1.

The side headings will be at least as detailed as the plan, though they may also include a number of other features, such as a breakdown of debtors and creditors and number of days outstanding.

It is vital that these reports should be in the same format as the phased plans. In some organizations, the control function is undertaken by the finance or accounts department and there is a separation from planning. This may lead to the irrational situation that planning and control information is produced on a different basis; not just the side headings but even the reporting units. This situation must be avoided as it completely stultifies the benefits of both. The systems must be totally integrated.

**Table 16.1**    Key factors: product 'P'

|  | | Actual | Target assumption | Actual |
|---|---|---|---|---|
| | | This period | | Last period |
| 1. | Customer markets | | | |
| | Market growth (volumes) | | | |
| | Market share (vol)    SBU | | | |
| | Competitor    A | | | |
| | Competitor    B | | | |
| | Price    SBU | | | |
| | Competitor    A | | | |
| | Competitor    B | | | |
| 2. | Suppliers | | | |
| | Raw materials prices    SBU | | | |
| | Competitor    A | | | |
| | Competitor    B | | | |
| 3. | Productivity | | | |
| | Employment costs/sales    SBU | | | |
| | Competitor    A | | | |
| | Competitor    B | | | |
| | Capacity utilization    SBU | | | |
| | Competitor    A | | | |
| | Competitor    B | | | |
| | Total output    SBU | | | |
| | Competitor    A | | | |
| | Competitor    B | | | |
| 4. | Financial market | | | |
| | Exchange rates | | | |
| | Overdraft rate | | | |

| Period | | | Cumalative | | | Full year | | |
|---|---|---|---|---|---|---|---|---|
| Plan | Actual | Prior Year | Plan | Actual | Prior Year | Plan | Estimate | Prior Year |

**Figure 16.1**    Monthly report headings

## Amending plans

In the above headings, a column for a full year's estimate is provided. This enables an up-to-date view to be given of the outcome for the full year without amending the plan. As a general rule, the annual plan should not be amended once it has been agreed. If it were possible to modify it for every change in external assumptions or other matter beyond management control, it would cease to fulfil its purpose of being a yardstick against which to measure performance. On the other hand, if some event has occurred which renders the plan meaningless, there is little to commend its continuing to be used as a target. In consequence, practical compromises between the two principles have to be adopted from time to time.

Thus, if a fire destroyed the company's factory and it was decided not to rebuild, but to buy the product in, this would represent such a major change that the original plan would be treated as at an end and a new one would have to be substituted. If, however, a major supplier's factory was burnt down, causing shortages and cost increases in raw materials, this would not warrant such a change. The management would have to exert their ingenuity to try to maintain their plan, particularly as the competition would most likely be in the same predicament. They would get sympathy and encouragement rather than concessions!

This does not mean that the danger signals are ignored at the higher level. As indicated, a latest estimate is to be given, even though the plan remains. From this and from discussion with the manager concerned, the chief executive will take the necessary precautions. The accountant will be sent off to see the bank manager well in advance of a cash crisis, or whatever else may be needed to avert a last minute panic.

### The chief executive and control

Though reports on performance are normally submitted monthly, there is no consequent need for meetings to take place with a similar regularity. There is nothing like a routine meeting to dull the edge of management. They should only be held when there is something to talk about and the more flexible chief executives can be in this, the more time they will be able to devote to the really important issues, and to keeping colleagues on their toes!

Their main enemy is time, particularly time to absorb all the information, and they will often rely to a degree on 'quick fixes'—just a few key items which tell them what is happening. These are important to keep abreast of events and are provided ahead of the full details chief executives will subsequently get from their staff and managers.

They may choose to use in their information pack, a display such as a 'Z' chart which gives them an instant picture of the progress of any business along whatever dimension they may choose to measure it.

An example of a 'Z' chart is given in Fig. 16.2; it is so called because of the typical appearance of the display, and it shows the profit of the business month by month. It is made up cumulatively; thus the display at six months can be seen by covering up the data for months 7 to 12. At that six months point, a

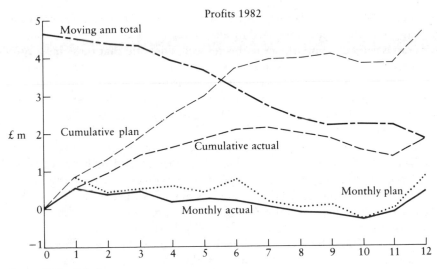

**Figure 16.2**   'Z' chart

reasonably alarming shortfall against plan was depicted. While the monthly actual against plan looked containable, this was not the message from the cumulative figures and the adverse situation was further pointed up by the moving annual total. Action needed to be taken and this was clear from the divergence of the diagonals in the 'Z', representing the cumulative position, right from the early periods in the year.

## The use of ratios

Another way of getting quickly to the heart of matters is by reviewing the critical ratios. The importance of a ratio is that it describes the structure of some part of the business. A change in a ratio means a change in structure. Thus, return on sales shows the relationship between sales and profit. An examination of this relationship is likely to show that the percentage value tends to reduce on the downside of the trade cycle and increase on the upside. This is not always so; business publishing is a low cost of entry activity, and in boom times it tends to get flooded with new entrants. This puts pressure on the margins of the more established operators. As the economy dips, however, many of the new entrants cannot survive the competition and advertisers will support the tried and trusted journals. This relieves some of the pressure on margins, though depressed volumes may have a countervailing effect on them.

Whatever the pattern, if the return on sales begins to show some uncharacteristic behaviour, this can be spotted quickly. Perhaps a month by month check on Conglom's IS division might have identified early the dramatic margin drop from 20 per cent in 1983 to 13 per cent in 1984.

There are many other appropriate ratios to scan which will reveal problems less apparent than those identified by examining the return on sales. Productivity ratios can be of importance in this respect. The ratio that is the most comprehensive in measuring performance is, however, ROTC. It encompasses both the profit and the balance sheet in that it measures profit as a proportion of fixed assets plus working capital. It is calculated before interest and tax or borrowings and cash, thus avoiding the distorting influence of financing on performance trends.

No single ratio, however, is adequate to give a full picture. ROTC can be pushed up by cutting back on growth, to produce quick benefits in earnings, but at the expense of the long-term profit generating capacity. Furthermore, ROTC may be at a constantly high level without generating any cash. The chief executive should, therefore, use among the 'quick-fix' figures, not only ROTC, but also changes in sales volumes and the period cash flow.

An additional use for ROTC is to enable comparison between different types of business. At the level of return on sales, the question has to be asked 'but is there some other feature of the business, like capital intensity which will nullify the beneficial/adverse effect of a high/low margin?'. ROTC is calculated after taking all trading profit and trading capital elements into account. It provides a yardstick for comparison of actual and potential profit between different sorts of business.

It has to be added that there are some businesses where ROTC does not work as a measure. Any service business that gets its cash in before it performs its side of the bargain is likely to have a negative capital employed. This is the case, for example, with trade shows. Broking firms, estate agents and similar businesses with very low capital intensity will have ROTCs up in the hundreds. They will have to choose alternative measures to judge performance. Perhaps return on sales is the best to use in such circumstances. This only underlines the reality that in running business, there are few hard and fast rules, and the judgement of experienced operators remains paramount.

## Investment control

In a small business, the chief executive will keep a tight control of all investment. As the size of the organization grows, some delegation of authority is necessary. In addition to regular monthly reporting against plan most organizations have *ad hoc* procedures for the control of capital expenditure and of acquisitions and disposals above a certain level. Indeed, where action could trigger the repayment of a loan (for example, where the asset to be sold is secured by a debenture) any such transaction would require central approvals.

The criteria against which the validity of a project is to be judged have been discussed in Chapter 9. The actual setting of ground rules for reporting is, however, quite a complex matter. A balance has to be kept between placing too many restrictions on individual managers, yet allowing an adequate assurance that nothing of importance is slipping through the net.

The following are some of the considerations to bear in mind. First, the level of expenditure up to which any subordinate manager may authorize a project should be fixed by reference to:

- the capability of that manager;
- the number of projects he or she is likely to have to deal with;
- the competition for funds from other parts of the business.

It is also very much a question of the management style of the organization concerned; some companies seek to exert a strong central control, while others are prepared to devolve a high level of responsibility.

An over-restrictive approach may, however, render the system unworkable and tend to no control, as top management seek to battle with an avalanche of paperwork that they have insufficient time to read. It was reported that, in the 'sixties, the Politburo in the Soviet Union retained the power to approve all projects in excess of \$1m.[2] It is not credible that such a system could operate at all in such a vast economic entity. Either the report was misleading or, in practice, some other mechanisms were used.

Second is the question of the extent to which projects not included in plans may be authorized. In most businesses, minor expenditure will not in any event be detailed. A lump sum will be included to cover all such matters and the problem of switching from one project to another does not arise. The only decision to be made in this context is where the cut-off occurs between major and minor projects. This again is a matter to be regulated by the factors mentioned above, i.e. competence, volume of projects and availability of resource.

So far as major projects are concerned, most businesses require that those not included in the plans should have independent justification and that all of them should be brought forward for approval. Others will, however, allow projects that are a direct substitute for those planned and that are within a manager's normal authority, to proceed on that manager's approval, without further authorization. Many alternative procedures are possible, but it is important that the overall planned expenditure should not be exceeded without the approval of the chief executive.

The following is a typical set of rules relating to levels of authorization:

From: Chief Executive, Conglom.
To: Chief Executive, Industrial Services Division.

### Capital expenditure authorization

Your division may proceed with any capital project included in its agreed business plan, without further approval from Conglom, provided that the total value of any such project does not exceed £200 000 and that you personally authorize any such project in excess of £20 000. [£20 000 is the level set by Conglom as the upper value limit of minor projects.]

Where you wish to substitute a new project for one included in the agreed business plan, you may do so on the above basis, with the substitution of an authorization limit of £100 000. You should report such change in your monthly report following your decision to do so.

Where you wish to invest in a project not covered above, any such proposal over the sum of £20 000 must be reported for approval by Conglom. In no circumstances is the total investment included in the agreed business plan to be exceeded without Conglom's approval.

## What expenditure is included

The next question to address is what expenditure is to be treated as part of the project. To be concerned with fixed assets alone is clearly not enough: in some cases, the working capital element may be much higher. Working capital, however, has a continuously changing value. When should the total project investment be struck, for the purposes of evaluating its acceptability? As a matter of practicality, the total spend may be treated as terminating either at the time the last fixed capital investment is made, or, if later, the time when the product is first introduced to the market.

Another difficulty arises in deciding whether a project is isolated or is to be treated, for evaluation and authorization limits, as one of a series. It is an easy option for a manager to evade seeking higher approval by splitting a project up into a series of smaller ones, each within his authority level. In the real world, however, the rule to apply is that any project that cannot stand alone to fulfil a tactical option must be combined with such others as are essential to such fulfilment.

In other words, if more money needs to be spent to launch a product, to achieve a cost reduction or to improve productivity in a particular way, that must be included. The total sum to be spent on redundancy, for example, should be included with the cost of new equipment which may bring this about. Furthermore, each of the improvements to be made to the production line should be added in. The object is to be clear that, after everything has been taken into consideration, the total project, together with the business to which it applies, is financially viable and that the resources are being properly used in line with business strategies.

Confusion can be introduced by including financing elements in the project costing. It is common to lease buildings or major items of plant. For a proper evaluation, however, the capital cost should be used for all such assets. The benefits of financing by leasing, borrowing or any other means may then be tested. Since these mechanisms may be affected by taxation, any project that only becomes feasible through their use should be considered with caution, though it is acceptable that credit should be taken for any government grants that may be receivable for a scheme.

In addition to the strategic and tactical evaluation of a project, it is necessary to assess the cash flow implications in detail. The approach to the calculations was considered in some detail in Chapter 9 and the topic is not considered further here.

## Conclusion

It has been said of some large corporations that their whole planning systems are little more than a mechanism for evaluating capital expenditure. While this may be a most important aspect of investment, especially for organizations with high capital intensity, it is evident from the foregoing discussions that it can only be part of the process of planning.

In concluding this chapter, the need for control in order to make sense of planning is again emphasized. In a proper system, the two functions are fused together, so that there is a constant interaction between, on the one hand, information coming in to confirm or modify the view of the state of the business and, on the other, decisions being made as to the actions to take. The way in which control is exerted is a matter of style. No general formats can be laid down for the whole process. What is important is that the chief executive and the management team should know what is going on and be able to act in the light of good information and advice. One of the most important features of any planning system is its ability to ensure that good information is readily available, in common format and focusing upon the critical issues.

## Notes

1. Royal Commission on Technical Instruction, London, 1882.
2. Paper presented by G. Shevchenko former USSR ambassador to the United Nations, to a conference arranged by Oxford Analytica at Oxford, 1984.

# 17

# Planning in practice

## A diversity of personal styles

It is evident that Jack Robinson and Sir James Forbes, CB, have to adopt different approaches to running their business. Plinmo and Conglom make very different demands on their chief executives. But this does not describe how these two men actually operate.

Consider some of the leading businessmen in Britain in 1984. Listed alphabetically, rather than in any order of precedence, this group would include Sir Michael Edwardes, Sir Owen Green, Sir John Harvey-Jones, Sir Alex Jarrett, Robert Maxwell, Sir John Raisman and 'Tiny' Rowlands. Each of these has his own individual approach and this individuality is multiplied throughout the commercial community by the number of chief executives.

Pity the poor planners, therefore, whose job it is to provide planning services. How are they to sort out what style is going to appeal to their boss? Admittedly this is a problem for all central staff, but strategic and tactical planning are both critical to the management of the business; planners are centre-stage in carrying out their rôle. They cannot take refuge behind expertise or have the opportunity to build a little cubby-hole for themselves into which they can withdraw from the idiosyncrasies of their chief.

## Organization and risk

The matrix in Table 17.1 is a not-too-serious attempt to make a crude classification that might help to illustrate the differing attitudes of chief executives to planning. It shows on one scale, the degree of structure that the CEO adopts in running the business. This dimension comprehends such factors as techniques, adequacy of information, quality of thinking and so on. It represents the continuum from strict regimentation to chaos. The other scale relates to risk-taking. How much of a gambler is the CEO? Will he or she take the plunge despite or because of the evidence? This continuum moves from total caution to total adventurism.

The labels attaching to the categories in the table are arbitrary and it would be misleading to pretend that this display is anything other than impressionistic. It is an imaginative, rather than scientific survey of types of manager. Its purpose is to point out how many different types of management styles there

**Table 17.1**   The chief executive as a planner

|  |  |  |  |  |
|---|---|---|---|---|
|  | High | Bureaucratic | Systematic | Militaristic |
| *Structure* | Medium | Incremental | Pragmatic | Speculative |
|  | Low | Squirearchical | Entrepreneurial | Buccaneer |
|  |  | Low | Medium | High |
|  |  |  | *RISK* |  |

appear to be, just looking at two dimensions. Armed with this understanding, planners should recognize that they must adapt their style to that of the chief executive. There is no one right way of planning to which they are obliged to adhere despite the requirements of their boss.

## Opponents of planning

Indeed, it has to be understood that unless planners have the approval and support of their chief executive, they will not be able to achieve anything. In the ant-heap of a commercial corporation there are too many competing interests. Unlike the ants, there is no genetic compulsion to act together and the goals of the individual may be very different to the goals of the organization. The sorts of opposition that occur include the following categories:

- *Alibi seekers*   There are some operating managers for whom the searchlight of a properly structured system sheds too much illumination on their activities for comfort. In answering for failures in their planning or managing, they prefer the obscurity of dark corners and the security of knowing that no-one else knows enough about the business to interrogate them seriously.
- *Wrinkled old retainers*   Many who have achieved success through experience will prefer to protect their advantage and their job by ensuring that only those who have served an extended apprenticeship may be admitted to the arcane mysteries of management.
- *High-fliers*   Those whose rewards come from the present system of remuneration according to the short-term goals of this year's (or even last year's) profit or cash flow will fight like cats to avoid the more considered approach implicit in planning, where strategic direction has an impact on take-home pay.

Machiavelli was right:

There is nothing more difficult to put in hand, more perilous to conduct, or more uncertain in its success, than to take the lead in the introduction of a new order of things, because the innovator has for enemies all those who have done well under the old conditions and lukewarm defenders in those who may do well under the new.

*The Prince*

For, taking the state of the planning art as it is at present, it is clear that there is plenty of room for planners to innovate in management methods, in information systems and in structures. And once this is accomplished in any organization, they must be agents for continually questioning the new order—a kind of corporate Maoist.

## The skills of the planner

What sort of skills should such an executive have? While planners in different organizations must operate according to different management styles they should not, nevertheless, ignore the information needs and methods for using information that have been discussed earlier. It only means that the way in which they communicate and manage the relationship with their corporate colleagues will vary from business to business.

The skills that the planner should command include the following:

- *Ability to communicate*   The capacity to provide information to those within the business who need it in a way that makes sense to them;
- *Ability to analyse*   The comprehension of statistical techniques, knowing which is right to use in any particular context and how to manipulate information appropriately;
- *Flexibility*   The ability to change the direction of thinking if the evidence is against what has currently been adopted as the strategic route;
- *Creativity*   Being able to think up new solutions and to stimulate others to do likewise;
- *Practicality*   The attitude that rejects perfection but demands competence.

### THE ABILITY TO COMMUNICATE

Communication is an obvious skill to demand of planners. They may be (or have within their team) the most brilliant analysts, but unless they can get the messages across, the time spent on analysis is wasted. Experience has shown that in promoting a project, as much attention should be paid to presentation as to investigation. Planners must understand how to facilitate approval for their plans. The following are a number of common sense rules to be used so far as occasion allows:

- Have round the table more people who support the proposal than are likely to oppose it; this may mean starting with a very small meeting, perhaps with the chief executive alone, though if they are astute, CEOs will probably avoid being cornered like this!

- Suit the presentation to the audience; if the purpose is to put across plans to managers who feel uncomfortable with the sophisticated approach, avoid a slick style, cut out references to techniques, use shabby acetates, rather than glossy 35mm slides, and allow plenty of time for intervention;
- Never overkill with information, whether by projecting on to a screen a mass of incomprehensible data or by overloading a document with too many figures and tables; not even a brilliant planner can cope with that amount of information.
- If an audience appears to be getting bored, cut the presentation short, if necessary undertaking to give a supplementary show to anyone who wants to take up the offer. Similarly, keep documents as short as possible and avoid discussion of strategic principles such as the merits of strengthening market share. The readers should know this already and if they do not, they are likely to be unimpressed!
- If the audience appears to be getting hostile, avoid a decision at all costs; there are few who have the strength of purpose to avoid deferring a decision if this is asked for, but many who will say 'no' if they are pulled on to a decision prematurely.

These are all fairly obvious suggestions. What is difficult to prescribe in positive terms is how to write the appropriate memorandum or make the right speech. This can only come through practice and it is something well worth studying. Since justice is not a feature to rely on in the commercial world, it has to be admitted that a superficial document or presentation that strikes the apt note is more likely to achieve success than a more thorough and scientific, but ill-presented one. This puts a high premium on communication skills, and indeed upon the integrity of the planner sponsoring such projects or plans.

UNDERSTANDING ANALYSIS

Conductors of an orchestra do not have to be able to play every instrument themselves. In the same way, it is not necessary for planners to be statisticians: the techniques discussed in Chapter 13 should all be familiar and they must know which to use for which purpose, but they do not actually have to do the analysis themselves.

Carrying the analogy further, it is often the case that the orchestra conductor will have a skill in playing a particular instrument—say the oboe. It would be ludicrous if, as a result, that conductor paid attention only to the oboe line in the score. Similarly, the planner may have knowledge of regression analysis or the PIMS programme, but it would be equally unprofessional to seek to resolve all business problems using these techniques alone.

Yet some newly appointed planning manager with a hang-up for particular methodologies may seek to turn the whole system hitherto adopted by his organization upside down for the sake of the exclusive adoption of some pet preferences. There is always value in having light directed upon a problem from a new angle, but those who believe that solely by the application of a single new technique are they going to solve the corporation's strategic issues are misled. Techniques do not solve strategic problems, they only structure information. Those who believe that they can produce answers that have necessarily eluded their predecessors merely by waving a magic matrix, should never be appointed to the job of planner at all.

Others on the list of undesirables as planners, are those who are prepared to take on the planning job as an interim measure between line appointments, with little interest other than to get back to the shop floor as soon as possible; others are put in just because the chief executive cannot find them appropriate posts at the time. Yet others seize the opportunity as a means to securing a power base and a stepping stone to the top. This last is probably an illusion, though a corner on information represents a very powerful political tool. To make the determination of strategy subject to such vagaries, a political shuttlecock for managers between operational appointments or executives jostling for power, is an irresponsible act.

## 'SOFT' SYSTEMS

It is worth commenting, in this discussion of the application of techniques that this chapter is in fact very much concerned with what are often called 'soft' systems. These very broadly are complementary approaches for problem solving in areas where strictly quantitative methods may not be effective. Since this book aims to deal with planning in a relatively simplified way, the emphasis has been on the 'hard', quantifying approach. Nevertheless, there is a whole spectrum of 'soft' techniques of considerable value to those acting as consultants, whether internally as planners, or externally as professional advisers. The present relative disrepute of strategic planning must owe something to the failure of planners to recognize the total 'people' environment within which they work and the importance of, at the least, competence in influencing their colleagues. It is to the analysis of this environment and of the cultural values of the individuals and groups with whom planners work that 'soft' systems are directed.

Corporate consultants/planners should be able, in particular, to analyse the power structure in order to optimize the chances of success. If they know who (or which caucus) makes the decisions, they recognize who their 'client' should be. To report to or work for any other group will be both frustrating and fruitless. This should not be interpreted as an invitation to adopt the cynical approach of certain consultants who, having wedged the foot in the door, ascertain where the power base resides in the organization and without any concern for the merits from a commercial point of view, formulate proposals that solely reflect the political aspirations of that power base. Such an attitude to consulting may prove lucrative, but it only weaves a non-existent suit of clothes for the corporate emperor. It is of no genuine use to the corporation itself, though it may be just what the project sponsor in that corporation is looking for.

FLEXIBILITY, CREATIVITY AND PRACTICALITY
Flexibility is a rare quality and should not be confused with an inability to reach decisions (which is all too common). The larger the organization, the less flexible it inevitably becomes. Many giant organizations have that characteristic of a supertanker which requires it to swing the wheel to change course long before the ship is anywhere near the rocks. Unhappily, this feature is not universally recognized. In such an environment, it is very easy for the planner to adopt a similarly inflexible attitude and say: 'We're doing pretty well at the moment and we can't go altering our strategies every five mintues.'

It is, however, the planner's task to be continually questioning what is being done, not necessarily in the expectation that strategies should change, but in case they might. This flexibility of mind should be allied with creative ability in an attempt to pierce the obscurity of the future and contemplate what may be if things go differently from plan assumptions. Not much more can be said about creativity; it is not a skill to be learned, tending to be innate, though those with it may be able to enhance through practice their natural abilities.

Finally, practicality. There is little different for the planner in this than for any other corporate executive. Commercial life is not about the best possible solution, but about achieving a regular flow of satisfactory transactions. Those who seek only the best solutions are likely to end up proposing no solutions at all. At the same time, this cannot be treated as a refuge for incompetence. There has to be a balance. The need to exercise skill in gathering, manipulating and presenting information in a way that assists the business in moving towards its objectives is re-emphasized. The work must be correctly focused and done thoroughly.

## Staffing the planning department
In concluding these comments on the practicalities of planning, there is the question of the size and staffing of the planning department. Again there can be a very wide variety of approaches to this. The tendency for industrial concentrates, where there is a very high level of common problems, is to focus effort through a central planning department. The major oil companies are examples of this. A conglomerate such as Conglom, however, will have to disperse its staff amongst individual business units as the markets on the supply and demand sides are very different and require individual study. It is only at the macroeconomic level that there is sufficient common interest amongst the individual activities of such an organization to justify a centralized approach.

The expertise that any planning department should be able to deploy (in addition to the individual qualities of the planner described earlier) are outlined below:

- *Economics*   Not just to forecast economic change, but also to scan the environment and assess information covering the social and political scenes as well as macro- and micro-markets; this covers the environmental part of the planning machine.
- *Accounting*   The language of business is very largely the language of accounting; accountants have to interpret the information available ultimately in profit and loss, balance sheet and cash flow terms and are concerned to see that information is put together in the right way; they play a major part in constructing the financial models and also are concerned with the operations part of the planning machine.
- *Systems*   Information and decisions cannot just be thrown together in a large pot in the hope that coherent strategies and management actions will emerge; the planning machine has to have a designer. The systems architect will also be concerned with the structural options for corporate strategy.
- *Programming*   If any part of the planning machine is to be run on computers (and even in small businesses nowadays it would be exceptional not to find one somewhere in the office), there must be programmers available to write the software.
- *Administration*   Behind all the clever stuff, there has to be a strong administrator to ensure that what needs to happen to keep the machine ticking over actually does happen.

These are the disciplines that need to be available, but it is not necessary that all should be maintained 'in-house'. It is certainly feasible to use external consultants for some of these tasks, particularly systems architecture and econometrics. Programmers may also be brought in on an *ad hoc* basis. Other functions may be combined. In a small organization, the accountant and administrator will be a single individual, who may well be the chief planner, too. The person who is responsible to the chief executive for the overall planning function must, however, have access to a wide variety of expertise and information, and must know when and how to use it and be able to recognize its quality. This paragon is the perfect planner.

# Conclusion

This discussion on practical business planning began with a description in Part 1 of the essential matters to think through in order to enable proper plans to be prepared. It considered in Part 2 where the necessary information might come from and how it could be used and this part ended with a review of how the planner had to operate in a real-life corporate situation.

Such a discussion can, however, only be an introduction to a topic so wide ranging as planning. To become an effective planner, an executive will have to be involved in actually doing it for a number of years. By that time, much of what has been written here will seem naive, many of the techniques old-fashioned. Nevertheless, the basic structure of objectives, strategies, tactics and finance should remain the way to approach business planning.

Even when practitioners have a reasonable amount of experience behind them, they still have to be wary about transporting their experience to other businesses, because each operates in such a different way. Businesses have a way of rejecting alien tissue. If, however, they recognize:

- the objectives of the new organization
- the aspirations and management style of their new chief executive
- the vested interests of their new colleagues
- the competencies of their own team

they may stand a fair chance of success.

# Appendix 1
# Conglom PLC and Plinmo Limited accounts

# Conglom: Annual business plans, 1980–82

## Schedule 1

*Currency:* £m

*Date:* 1 Nov. 79

*Business plan, 1980–82: Conglom summary*

| | | Actual | | | | Original plan | Estimate as at period 8 | Plan | | |
|---|---|---|---|---|---|---|---|---|---|---|
| | | 1975 | 1976 | 1977 | 1978 | 1979 | 1979 | 1980 | 1981 | 1982 |
| | | (1) | (2) | (3) | (4) | (5) | (6) | (7) | (8) | (9) |
| Total external sales | (1) | 35.0 | 49.4 | 55.5 | 58.2 | 66.5 | 66.8 | 75.7 | 83.5 | 89.7 |
| Trading profit | (2) | 1.6 | 4.3 | 5.0 | 2.7 | 4.8 | 5.2 | 7.1 | 8.6 | 10.1 |
| Depreciation | (3) | 0.8 | 0.8 | 1.0 | 1.2 | 1.5 | 1.2 | 1.6 | 1.8 | 2.2 |
| Fixed-capital expenditure | (4) | 1.2 | 1.0 | 2.5 | 3.2 | 2.9 | 2.7 | 3.1 | 2.6 | 3.4 |
| Trading cash flow | (5) | 1.0 | 3.7 | 1.2 | (0.9) | 2.7 | 2.1 | 5.2 | 6.7 | 8.1 |
| Fixed assets NBA | (6) | 9.4 | 10.0 | 11.5 | 13.5 | 14.9 | 15.0 | 16.5 | 17.3 | 18.5 |
| Working capital | (7) | 7.7 | 8.0 | 10.3 | 11.9 | 12.6 | 13.5 | 13.9 | 15.0 | 15.8 |
| Trading capital | (8) | 17.1 | 18.0 | 21.8 | 25.4 | 27.5 | 28.5 | 30.4 | 32.3 | 34.3 |
| Ratios (%) | | | | | | | | | | |
| Profit margin | (9) | 5 | 9 | 9 | 5 | 7 | 8 | 9 | 10 | 11 |
| Fixed-capital intensity | (10) | 27 | 20 | 21 | 23 | 22 | 23 | 22 | 21 | 21 |
| Working capital/sales | (11) | 22 | 16 | 19 | 20 | 19 | 20 | 18 | 18 | 18 |
| ROTC | (12) | 9 | 24 | 23 | 11 | 17 | 18 | 23 | 27 | 29 |

# Schedule 2

*Currency:* £m                                                              *Date*: 1 Nov. 79

*Business plan, 1980–82: Cash flow*

|  |  | Actual | | Original plan | Estimate as at period 8 | Plan | | |
|---|---|---|---|---|---|---|---|---|
|  |  | 1977 | 1978 | 1979 | 1979 | 1980 | 1981 | 1982 |
|  |  | (1) | (2) | (3) | (4) | (5) | (6) | (7) |
| Trading profit | (1) | 5.0 | 2.7 | 4.8 | 5.2 | 7.1 | 8.6 | 10.1 |
| Depreciation | (2) | 1.0 | 1.2 | 1.5 | 1.2 | 1.6 | 1.8 | 2.2 |
| Inflow from trading | (3) | 6.0 | 3.9 | 6.3 | 6.4 | 8.7 | 10.4 | 12.3 |
| Capital expenditure | (4) | 2.5 | 3.2 | 2.9 | 2.7 | 3.1 | 2.6 | 3.4 |
| Working capital movement | (5) | 2.3 | 1.6 | 0.7 | 1.6 | 0.4 | 1.1 | 0.8 |
| Trading cash flow | (6) | 1.2 | (0.9) | 2.7 | 2.1 | 5.2 | 6.7 | 8.1 |
| Net group interest | (7) | (1.0) | (1.2) | (2.0) | (1.8) | (1.1) | (0.4) | (0.1) |
| Dividends | (8) | (0.7) | (0.7) | (0.7) | (0.7) | (1.0) | (1.0) | (1.0) |
| Taxation (paid)/received | (9) | (1.1) | (0.3) | 0.0 | 0.0 | 0.0 | (1.7) | (4.0) |
| Total cash flow | (10) | (1.6) | (3.1) | 0.0 | (0.4) | 3.1 | 3.6 | 3.0 |
| Opening net long- and short-term borrowings | (11) | 7.2 | 8.8 | 11.9 | 11.9 | 12.3 | 9.2 | 5.6 |
| Movement on long-term borrowings | (12) | 0.0 | 0.0 | (0.8) | (0.8) | 1.8 | 0.0 | 0.0 |
| Movement on short-term borrowings | (13) | 1.6 | 3.1 | 0.8 | 1.2 | (4.9) | (3.6) | (3.0) |
| Closing net long- and short-term borrowings | (14) | 8.8 | 11.9 | 11.9 | 12.3 | 9.2 | 5.6 | 2.6 |

## Schedule 3

*Currency*: £m                                                            *Date*: 1 Nov. 79

*Business plan, 1980–82: Balance sheet*

|  |  | Actual | | Original plan | Estimate as at period 8 | Plan | | |
|---|---|---|---|---|---|---|---|---|
|  |  | 1977 | 1978 | 1979 | 1979 | 1980 | 1981 | 1982 |
|  |  | (1) | (2) | (3) | (4) | (5) | (6) | (7) |
| Fixed assets— | | | | | | | | |
| closing NBA | (1) | 11.5 | 13.5 | 14.9 | 15.0 | 16.5 | 17.3 | 18.5 |
| Working capital | (2) | 10.3 | 11.9 | 12.6 | 13.5 | 13.9 | 15.0 | 15.8 |
| Trading capital | (3) | 21.8 | 25.4 | 27.5 | 28.5 | 30.4 | 32.3 | 34.3 |
| Goodwill | (4) | 4.1 | 4.1 | 4.1 | 4.1 | 4.1 | 4.1 | 4.1 |
| Gross cap. emp. | (5) | 25.9 | 29.5 | 31.6 | 32.6 | 34.5 | 36.4 | 38.4 |
| Net short-term | | | | | | | | |
| borrowings | (6) | 2.8 | 5.9 | 6.7 | 7.1 | 2.2 | (1.4) | (4.4) |
| Long-term | | | | | | | | |
| borrowings | (7) | 6.0 | 6.0 | 5.2 | 5.2 | 7.0 | 7.0 | 7.0 |
| Taxation | (8) | 0.3 | (1.0) | 0.0 | (0.1) | 1.7 | 4.0 | 4.1 |
| Share capital | (9) | 6.0 | 6.0 | 6.0 | 6.0 | 6.0 | 6.0 | 6.0 |
| Opening reserves | (10) | 7.8 | 10.8 | 12.6 | 12.6 | 14.4 | 17.6 | 20.8 |
| Retained profit | (11) | 3.0 | 1.8 | 1.1 | 1.8 | 3.2 | 3.2 | 4.9 |
| HCA financing | (12) | 25.9 | 29.5 | 31.6 | 32.6 | 34.5 | 36.4 | 38.4 |
| Debt | (13) | 8.8 | 11.9 | 11.9 | 12.3 | 9.2 | 5.6 | 2.6 |
| Equity | (14) | 12.7 | 14.5 | 15.6 | 16.3 | 19.5 | 22.7 | 27.6 |
| D/E ratio (%) | (15) | 69 | 82 | 76 | 75 | 47 | 25 | 9 |

# Schedule 4

*Currency*: £m                                                                 *Date*: 1 Nov. 79

*Business plan, 1981–82: Sales and profits*

|  |  | Actual | | Original Plan | Estimate as at period 8 |  | Plan | |
|  |  | 1977 | 1978 | 1979 | 1979 | 1980 | 1981 | 1982 |
|---|---|---|---|---|---|---|---|---|
|  |  | (1) | (2) | (3) | (4) | (5) | (6) | (7) |
| Total sales | (1) | 56.1 | 58.8 | 67.1 | 67.5 | 76.6 | 84.4 | 90.7 |
| Inter-group sales | (2) | (0.6) | (0.6) | (0.6) | (0.7) | (0.9) | (0.9) | (1.0) |
| Total external sales | (3) | 55.5 | 58.2 | 66.5 | 66.8 | 75.7 | 83.5 | 89.7 |
| Trading profit | (4) | 5.0 | 2.7 | 4.8 | 5.2 | 7.1 | 8.6 | 10.1 |
| Net interest | (5) | (1.0) | (1.2) | (2.0) | (1.8) | (1.1) | (0.4) | (0.1) |
| Profit before tax | (6) | 4.0 | 1.5 | 2.8 | 3.4 | 6.0 | 8.2 | 10.0 |
| Taxation | (7) | (0.3) | 1.0 | (1.0) | (0.9) | (1.8) | (4.0) | (4.1) |
| Profit after tax | (8) | 3.7 | 2.5 | 1.8 | 2.5 | 4.2 | 4.2 | 5.9 |
| Dividends | (9) | (0.7) | (0.7) | (0.7) | (0.7) | (1.0) | (1.0) | (1.0) |
| Retained profit | (10) | 3.0 | 1.8 | 1.1 | 1.8 | 3.2 | 3.2 | 4.9 |

# Schedule 5

Industrial Services Limited (£m)

| | 1975 | Actual 1976 | 1977 | 1978 | Original plan 1979 | Latest estimate 1979 | 1980 | Plan 1981 | 1982 |
|---|---|---|---|---|---|---|---|---|---|
| *Business parameters* | | | | | | | | | |
| Total sales external | | | | | | | | | |
| to activity | 11.1 | 13.9 | 14.8 | 16.5 | 19.2 | 20.1 | 24.0 | 27.2 | 30.2 |
| Sales external to group | 10.7 | 13.3 | 14.2 | 15.9 | 18.6 | 19.4 | 23.1 | 26.3 | 29.2 |
| Activity profit | 1.2 | 2.0 | 2.0 | 2.3 | 2.7 | 3.0 | 3.6 | 4.2 | 4.8 |
| Activity cash flow | 0.7 | 1.8 | 1.8 | 1.6 | 1.3 | 1.3 | 2.0 | 3.1 | 3.7 |
| Average working capital | 1.9 | 2.1 | 2.2 | 2.4 | 3.1 | 3.5 | 4.4 | 5.0 | 5.5 |
| Average inventories | 1.1 | 1.2 | 1.2 | 1.3 | 1.3 | 1.6 | 1.9 | 2.1 | 2.4 |
| Fixed assets at cost | 2.8 | 3.0 | 3.4 | 4.1 | 5.5 | 5.2 | 6.5 | 7.7 | 9.1 |
| Fixed assets NBA | 1.6 | 1.7 | 2.0 | 2.5 | 3.3 | 3.2 | 4.1 | 4.7 | 5.5 |
| Depreciation HCA | 0.1 | 0.1 | 0.2 | 0.3 | 0.4 | 0.3 | 0.4 | 0.6 | 0.7 |
| Depreciation CCA | 0.4 | 0.4 | 0.5 | 0.6 | 0.9 | 0.7 | 0.9 | 1.1 | 1.3 |
| Fixed-capital expenditure | 0.2 | 0.2 | 0.5 | 0.8 | 1.2 | 1.0 | 1.3 | 1.2 | 1.4 |
| Employment costs | 2.5 | 2.9 | 3.3 | 4.0 | 4.4 | 4.8 | 5.6 | 6.4 | 7.1 |
| Energy costs | 0.1 | 0.2 | 0.2 | 0.2 | 0.2 | 0.2 | 0.2 | 0.2 | 0.3 |
| Raw materials costs | 6.0 | 7.4 | 7.3 | 7.8 | 9.1 | 9.2 | 11.2 | 12.7 | 14.0 |
| Other charges | 1.2 | 1.3 | 1.8 | 1.9 | 2.4 | 2.6 | 3.0 | 3.1 | 3.3 |
| Extraordinary items | 0.0 | 0.0 | 0.0 | 0.0 | 0.0 | 0.0 | 0.0 | 0.0 | 0.0 |
| Number of employees | 700 | 686 | 671 | 671 | 671 | 671 | 657 | 657 | 660 |
| *Indices and ratios* | | | | | | | | | |
| Volume index | 75 | 85 | 84 | 90 | 98 | 96 | 100 | 104 | 108 |
| ROTC | 35.1% | 53.6% | 49.1% | 46.1% | 42.8% | 44.3% | 42.6% | 43.3% | 43.9% |
| Profit margin | 11.1% | 14.7% | 13.8% | 13.8% | 14.1% | 14.8% | 15.1% | 15.5% | 16.0% |
| Working capital/sales | 17.4% | 15.4% | 14.6% | 14.7% | 16.0% | 17.6% | 18.5% | 18.5% | 18.3% |
| Capacity utilization | 76.1% | 82.7% | 86.0% | 94.4% | 97.2% | 99.9% | 101.6% | 97.3% | 95.0% |

# Schedule 6

Consumer Services Limited (£m)

| | 1975 | Actual 1976 | 1977 | 1978 | Original plan 1979 | Latest estimate 1979 | 1980 | Plan 1981 | 1982 |
|---|---|---|---|---|---|---|---|---|---|
| *Business parameters* | | | | | | | | | |
| Total sales external to activity | 6.2 | 7.6 | 9.4 | 11.1 | 12.6 | 13.3 | 15.5 | 17.2 | 18.6 |
| Sales external to group | 6.2 | 7.6 | 9.4 | 11.1 | 12.6 | 13.3 | 15.5 | 17.2 | 18.6 |
| Activity profit | 0.3 | 0.9 | 1.5 | 1.6 | 1.5 | 1.9 | 2.0 | 2.3 | 2.5 |
| Activity cash flow | 0.3 | 0.9 | 1.4 | 1.5 | 0.9 | 0.8 | 1.3 | 2.0 | 2.5 |
| Average working capital | 0.4 | 0.5 | 0.7 | 0.8 | 0.8 | 1.4 | 1.4 | 1.6 | 1.6 |
| Average inventories | 0.3 | 0.3 | 0.4 | 0.5 | 0.5 | 0.6 | 0.6 | 0.7 | 0.7 |
| Fixed assets at cost | 0.6 | 0.6 | 0.7 | 0.9 | 1.5 | 1.5 | 2.4 | 2.7 | 3.0 |
| Fixed assets NBA | 0.3 | 0.3 | 0.4 | 0.5 | 1.0 | 1.0 | 1.7 | 1.8 | 1.9 |
| Depreciation HCA | 0.1 | 0.1 | 0.1 | 0.1 | 0.2 | 0.1 | 0.2 | 0.2 | 0.3 |
| Depreciation CCA | M* | 0.1 | 0.1 | 0.1 | 0.2 | 0.2 | 0.3 | 0.3 | 0.3 |
| Fixed-capital expenditure | 0.1 | 0.1 | 0.2 | 0.2 | 0.7 | 0.7 | 0.9 | 0.4 | 0.4 |
| Employment costs | 1.7 | 1.9 | 2.2 | 2.7 | 3.1 | 3.3 | 4.0 | 4.3 | 4.7 |
| Energy costs | 0.1 | 0.1 | 0.1 | 0.1 | 0.1 | 0.1 | 0.1 | 0.1 | 0.2 |
| Raw materials costs | 3.3 | 3.7 | 4.4 | 5.3 | 6.2 | 6.3 | 7.4 | 8.1 | 8.7 |
| Other charges | 0.7 | 0.9 | 1.1 | 1.3 | 1.5 | 1.6 | 1.8 | 2.2 | 2.2 |
| Extraordinary items | 0.0 | 0.0 | 0.0 | 0.0 | 0.0 | 0.0 | 0.0 | 0.0 | 0.0 |
| Number of employees | 455 | 462 | 471 | 489 | 515 | 515 | 515 | 515 | 516 |
| *Indices and ratios* | | | | | | | | | |
| Volume index | 77 | 80 | 88 | 97 | 103 | 102 | 100 | 99 | 99 |
| ROTC | 48.0% | 114.0% | 136.8% | 130.7% | 86.2% | 77.8% | 64.1% | 68.5% | 73.4% |
| Profit margin | 5.5% | 12.3% | 15.9% | 14.8% | 12.0% | 14.0% | 12.8% | 13.4% | 13.6% |
| Working capital/sales | 7.1% | 6.8% | 7.5% | 7.2% | 6.2% | 10.4% | 9.3% | 9.3% | 8.4% |
| Capacity utilization | M* | M* | M* | M* | M* | M* | M* | M* | M* |

* M denotes data missing or omitted.

# Schedule 7

Consumer Manufacturers BV (D. Fl. m)

|  | Actual | | | | Original plan | Latest estimate | | Plan | |
|  | 1975 | 1976 | 1977 | 1978 | 1979 | 1979 | 1980 | 1981 | 1982 |
|---|---|---|---|---|---|---|---|---|---|
| *Business parameters* | | | | | | | | | |
| Total sales external | | | | | | | | | |
| to activity | 21.2 | 23.0 | 23.7 | 25.2 | 30.2 | 32.1 | 35.4 | 39.6 | 43.5 |
| Sales external to group | 21.2 | 23.0 | 23.7 | 25.2 | 30.2 | 32.1 | 35.4 | 39.6 | 43.5 |
| Activity profit | (0.7) | (0.9) | (1.8) | (4.8) | (1.5) | (1.4) | 1.3 | 2.7 | 4.1 |
| Activity cash flow | (2.7) | (0.7) | (5.2) | (14.0) | (2.4) | (1.0) | 0.4 | 2.4 | 3.0 |
| Average working capital | 3.5 | 3.4 | 3.5 | 5.6 | 7.6 | 5.8 | 7.0 | 7.6 | 8.3 |
| Average inventories | 4.4 | 4.7 | 7.7 | 7.8 | 7.6 | 6.0 | 6.5 | 6.9 | 7.3 |
| Fixed assets at cost | 27.1 | 26.7 | 30.8 | 38.4 | 40.8 | 42.4 | 44.3 | 46.9 | 49.5 |
| Fixed assets NBA | 12.1 | 13.2 | 15.5 | 20.7 | 20.8 | 20.2 | 19.9 | 19.6 | 20.0 |
| Depreciation HCA | 2.0 | 2.1 | 1.7 | 2.1 | 2.4 | 2.2 | 2.4 | 2.5 | 2.7 |
| Depreciation CCA | 2.1 | 2.6 | 2.8 | 3.0 | 2.3 | 2.5 | 3.1 | 3.7 | 4.3 |
| Fixed-capital expenditure | 3.8 | 2.0 | 5.0 | 7.1 | 2.5 | 1.7 | 2.1 | 2.2 | 3.0 |
| Employment costs | 10.9 | 11.2 | 12.8 | 14.2 | 11.7 | 12.4 | 13.5 | 14.5 | 15.6 |
| Energy costs | 1.6 | 2.4 | 2.8 | 2.8 | 2.8 | 3.2 | 3.6 | 3.6 | 4.0 |
| Raw materials costs | 2.8 | 2.6 | 3.2 | 3.7 | 4.7 | 4.5 | 4.9 | 5.1 | 5.4 |
| Other charges | 4.6 | 5.6 | 5.0 | 7.2 | 10.1 | 11.2 | 9.7 | 11.2 | 11.7 |
| Extraordinary items | 0.0 | 0.0 | 0.0 | 2.1 | 0.0 | 0.0 | 0.0 | 0.0 | 0.0 |
| Number of employees | 522 | 504 | 528 | 552 | 426 | 420 | 414 | 414 | 414 |
| *Indices and ratios* | | | | | | | | | |
| Volume index | 73 | 75 | 80 | 91 | 94 | 99 | 100 | 102 | 103 |
| ROTC | (4.2%) | (5.4%) | (9.7%) | (26.3%) | (5.3%) | (5.2%) | 4.7% | 10.0% | 14.5% |
| Profit margin | (3.1%) | (3.9%) | (7.8%) | (27.5%) | (5.0%) | (4.2%) | 3.6% | 6.9% | 9.4% |
| Working capital/sales | 16.4% | 14.8% | 14.8% | 22.1% | 25.2% | 18.0% | 19.6% | 19.2% | 19.2% |
| Capacity utilization | 88.0% | 81.9% | 97.2% | 94.1% | 100.0% | 94.9% | 100.0% | 100.0% | 100.0% |

# Schedule 8

Industrial Manufacturers Limited (£m)

| | | Actual | | | Original plan | Latest estimate | | Plan | |
|---|---|---|---|---|---|---|---|---|---|
| | 1975 | 1976 | 1977 | 1978 | 1979 | 1979 | 1980 | 1981 | 1982 |
| *Business parameters* | | | | | | | | | |
| Total sales external to activity | 14.3 | 23.6 | 26.4 | 25.5 | 28.3 | 26.6 | 28.4 | 30.3 | 31.1 |
| Sales external to group | 14.3 | 23.6 | 26.4 | 25.5 | 28.3 | 26.6 | 28.4 | 30.3 | 31.1 |
| Activity profit | 0.2 | 1.6 | 1.9 | 0.4 | 1.0 | 0.6 | 1.2 | 1.4 | 1.8 |
| Activity cash flow | 0.2 | 1.7 | (0.5) | (0.8) | 1.1 | 0.2 | 1.9 | 1.0 | 1.2 |
| Average working capital | 5.7 | 5.6 | 7.7 | 8.7 | 8.3 | 8.8 | 7.9 | 8.2 | 8.4 |
| Average inventories | 7.0 | 8.0 | 10.2 | 11.2 | 10.6 | 11.4 | 10.2 | 10.5 | 10.8 |
| Fixed assets at cost | 8.8 | 9.1 | 9.8 | 10.4 | 10.8 | 11.0 | 11.4 | 11.9 | 12.7 |
| Fixed assets NBA | 5.3 | 5.2 | 5.6 | 5.7 | 5.8 | 6.0 | 6.0 | 6.1 | 6.4 |
| Depreciation HCA | 0.2 | 0.2 | 0.3 | 0.3 | 0.3 | 0.3 | 0.4 | 0.4 | 0.5 |
| Depreciation CCA | 0.4 | 0.5 | 0.5 | 0.6 | 0.7 | 0.7 | 0.8 | 0.9 | 0.9 |
| Fixed-capital expenditure | 0.2 | 0.3 | 0.6 | 0.5 | 0.4 | 0.6 | 0.4 | 0.5 | 0.8 |
| Employment costs | 4.2 | 5.2 | 6.1 | 6.8 | 7.2 | 7.8 | 8.3 | 8.6 | 9.2 |
| Energy costs | 1.4 | 2.0 | 2.4 | 2.5 | 2.7 | 2.9 | 3.2 | 3.7 | 4.1 |
| Raw materials costs | 5.3 | 8.8 | 9.8 | 9.9 | 11.0 | 10.4 | 11.0 | 11.8 | 12.3 |
| Other charges | 3.0 | 5.8 | 5.9 | 5.6 | 6.1 | 4.6 | 4.3 | 4.4 | 3.2 |
| Extraordinary items | 0.0 | 0.0 | 0.0 | 0.0 | 0.0 | 0.0 | 0.0 | 0.0 | 0.0 |
| Number of employees | 1396 | 1481 | 1478 | 1451 | 1410 | 1440 | 1400 | 1350 | 1350 |
| *Indices and ratios* | | | | | | | | | |
| Volume index | 84 | 120 | 122 | 108 | 110 | 103 | 100 | 97 | 94 |
| ROTC | 1.8% | 14.8% | 14.3% | 2.8% | 7.1% | 4.1% | 8.6% | 9.8% | 12.2% |
| Profit margin | 1.4% | 6.8% | 7.2% | 1.6% | 3.5% | 2.3% | 4.2% | 4.6% | 5.8% |
| Working capital/sales | 39.9% | 23.7% | 29.2% | 34.1% | 29.3% | 33.1% | 27.8% | 27.1% | 27.0% |
| Capacity utilization | 64.0% | 90.0% | 92.0% | 82.0% | 93.0% | 78.0% | 76.0% | 73.0% | 71.0% |

**Plinmo Limited: Pro-forma profit and loss account**

| £'000s | Year 1 | 2 | 3 | 4 | 5 |
|---|---|---|---|---|---|
| Total sales | 1925 | 2231 | 2490 | 2493 | 2604 |
| Direct costs: | | | | | |
|   employment | 218 | 258 | 283 | 366 | 391 |
|   energy | 51 | 61 | 67 | 68 | 66 |
|   raw materials | 576 | 652 | 831 | 852 | 903 |
| Gross profit | 1080 | 1260 | 1309 | 1207 | 1244 |
| Indirect costs: | | | | | |
|   depreciation | 98 | 111 | 128 | 145 | 201 |
|   other overhead | 570 | 641 | 684 | 730 | 728 |
| Trading profit | 412 | 508 | 497 | 332 | 315 |
| Financial items: | | | | | |
|   interest | 40 | 43 | 18 | 20 | 54 |
|   taxation | 125 | 227 | 201 | 24 | 45 |
|   dividend | 100 | 100 | 100 | 100 | 100 |
| Retained earnings | 147 | 138 | 178 | 188 | 116 |

**Plinmo Limited: Framework balance sheet**

| £'000s | Year 1 | | 2 | | 3 | | 4 | | 5 | |
|---|---|---|---|---|---|---|---|---|---|---|
| Fixed assets | | 745 | | 753 | | 823 | | 1088 | | 1260 |
| Working capital: | | | | | | | | | | |
|   stocks and WIP | 370 | | 424 | | 469 | | 489 | | 498 | |
|   debtors | 385 | | 436 | | 511 | | 507 | | 598 | |
|   creditors | (290) | | (346) | | (359) | | (350) | | (405) | |
| | | 465 | | 514 | | 621 | | 646 | | 691 |
| Trading capital | | 1210 | | 1267 | | 1444 | | 1734 | | 1951 |
| Other payables | | | | | | | | | | |
|   (tax etc.) | | (125) | | (230) | | (204) | | (28) | | (49) |
| Cash | | 9 | | 55 | | 30 | | 5 | | 3 |
| Total assets | | 1094 | | 1092 | | 1270 | | 1711 | | 1905 |
| Borrowings: | | | | | | | | | | |
|   9% loan stock | | 250 | | 250 | | 250 | | 250 | | 250 |
|   Overdraft and | | | | | | | | | | |
|     short-term loans | | 145 | | 5 | | 5 | | 258 | | 336 |
| Shareholders interests: | | | | | | | | | | |
|   share capital | | 300 | | 300 | | 300 | | 300 | | 300 |
|   profit and loss a/c | | 399 | | 537 | | 715 | | 903 | | 1019 |
| | | 1094 | | 1092 | | 1270 | | 1711 | | 1905 |

# Appendix 2
# Specimen business plan schedules

*ACTIVITY SCHEDULE*       *ACTIVITY*      *CURRENCY*
*19  /  BUDGET*                    *DATE*

| | Row no. | | Actual | | | Original Plan | Est.as at period | Budget |
|---|---|---|---|---|---|---|---|---|
| | Year | | | | | | | |
| Total sales | 1 | | | | | | | |
| Employment costs | 2 | | | | | | | |
| Raw material costs | 3 | | | | | | | |
| Depreciation HCA | 4 | | | | | | | |
| Gross profit | 5 | | | | | | | |
| Overheads | 6 | | | | | | | |
| Activity profit HCA | 7 | | | | | | | |
| Activity cash flow | 8 | | | | | | | |
| Non-operational items | 9 | | | | | | | |
| Average working capital | 10 | | | | | | | |
| Year-end working capital | 11 | | | | | | | |
| Average stocks | 12 | | | | | | | |
| Fixed assets HCA | 13 | | | | | | | |
| Capital expenditure | 14 | | | | | | | |
| Depreciation CCA | 15 | | | | | | | |
| Activity trading capital | 16 | | | | | | | |
| Excess cost | 17 | | | | | | | |
| Av. no. of employees | 18 | | | | | | | |
| Y/E no. of employees | 19 | | | | | | | |
| *Ratios* | | | | | | | | |
| Materials price index* | 20 | | | | | 100 | | |
| Volume index | 21 | | | | | 100 | | |
| Market growth index* | 22 | | | | | 100 | | |
| Market share | 23 | | | | | | | |
| Act. capacity utilization | 24 | | | | | | | |
| Gross margin | 25 | | | | | | | |
| Employment costs/sales | 26 | | | | | | | |
| Activity profit/sales | 27 | | | | | | | |
| Working capital/sales | 28 | | | | | | | |
| Activity ROTC HCA | 29 | | | | | | | |
| Activity ROI | 30 | | | | | | | |

*If past year's data not available, this past data may be omitted.

This format is for a one-year budget. If it is to be used for a 3-year plan, the final column should be extended to conform to the following schedules.

*DIVISION*
*CURRENCY*

*DATE*

*BUSINESS PLAN 19   /*
*CASH FLOW*

| | | Actual | Original plan | Estimate as at period | Plan | | |
|---|---|---|---|---|---|---|---|
| Year | | 1 | 2 | 3 | 4 | 5 | 6 | 7 |
| Row no | | | | | | | | |
| Trading profit | 1 | | | | | | | |
| Depreciation | 2 | | | | | | | |
| Asset disposals @ NBA | 3 | | | | | | | |
| Non-trading items | 4 | | | | | | | |
| Inflow from trading | 5 | | | | | | | |
| Capital expenditure | 6 | | | | | | | |
| Working capital movement | 7 | | | | | | | |
| Trading cash flow | 8 | | | | | | | |
| Transfers of investments–intercompany | 9 | | | | | | | |
| Acquisition costs | 10 | | | | | | | |
| Divestment proceeds | 11 | | | | | | | |
| Cash flow before financing | 12 | | | | | | | |
| Net group interest | 13 | | | | | | | |
| External interest: | | | | | | | | |
| received | 14 | | | | | | | |
| paid | 15 | | | | | | | |
| Dividends from: | | | | | | | | |
| associates | 16 | | | | | | | |
| subsidiaries | 17 | | | | | | | |
| Dividends to: | | | | | | | | |
| parent co. | 18 | | | | | | | |
| minorities | 19 | | | | | | | |
| Movement on other Group balances | 20 | | | | | | | |
| Taxation (paid)/received | 21 | | | | | | | |
| Other cash movement | 22 | | | | | | | |
| Total cash flow | 23 | | | | | | | |
| Opening net long- and short-term borrowings | 24 | | | | | | | |
| Long-term: new loans | 25 | | | | | | | |
| redemptions | 26 | | | | | | | |
| Movement on short-term borrowings | 27 | | | | | | | |
| Total cash flow | 28 | | | | | | | |
| Balances on acquisitions/disposals | 29 | | | | | | | |
| Exchange differences | 30 | | | | | | | |
| Closing net long- and short-term borrowings | 31 | | | | | | | |

*DIVISION*
*CURRENCY*

*DATE*

*BUSINESS PLAN 19    /*
*BALANCE SHEET*

| | Year | Actual | | Original plan | Est. as at period | Plan | | |
|---|---|---|---|---|---|---|---|---|
| | | 1 | 2 | 3 | 4 | 5 | 6 | 7 |
| | Row no. | | | | | | | |
| Fixed assets – closing NBA | 1 | | | | | | | |
| Working capital | 2 | | | | | | | |
| Trading capital | 3 | | | | | | | |
| Non-trading items | 4 | | | | | | | |
| Investments in subs | 5 | | | | | | | |
| Investments other | 6 | | | | | | | |
| Associates | 7 | | | | | | | |
| Capital employed | 8 | | | | | | | |
| Goodwill | 9 | | | | | | | |
| HCA gross cap. emp. | 10 | | | | | | | |
| Net short-term borrowings: external | 11 | | | | | | | |
| intercompany | 12 | | | | | | | |
| Long-term borrowings | 13 | | | | | | | |
| Taxation current | 14 | | | | | | | |
| deferred | 15 | | | | | | | |
| Other Group balances | 16 | | | | | | | |
| Outside shareholders | 17 | | | | | | | |
| Share capital | 18 | | | | | | | |
| Share premium | 19 | | | | | | | |
| Opening reserves | 20 | | | | | | | |
| HCA retained profit | 21 | | | | | | | |
| Exchange difference | 22 | | | | | | | |
| Other movements | 23 | | | | | | | |
| Closing shareholders funds | 24 | | | | | | | |
| HCA financing | 25 | | | | | | | |

SCHEDULE P4

DIVISION
CURRENCY

DATE

BUSINESS PLAN 19    /
CAPITAL EXPENDITURE

| | Phasing of expenditure | | | | | | |
|---|---|---|---|---|---|---|---|
| | Prior years | | | | | Post | Total |
| Year | 1 | 2 | 3 | 4 | 5 | 6 | 7 |
| Major projects | | | | | | | |
| | | | | | | | |
| Minor projects | | | | | | | |
| Total capital expenditure | | | | | | | |

*DIVISION*
*CURRENCY*

*SCHEDULE P5*

*DATE*

*BUSINESS PLAN 19    /*
*BUSINESS ACTIVITY SUMMARY*

| | Original Plan | Est. as at period 8 | | Plan | |
|---|---|---|---|---|---|
| Year | 1 | 2 | 3 | 4 | 5 |
| *Total sales* Per activity schedules* | | | | | |
| Other activities | | | | | |
| Total | | | | | |
| *Activity profit* Per activity schedules* | | | | | |
| Other activities Total H.Q. costs Total non-operational items | | | | | |
| Divisional trading profit | | | | | |

*Nominate activities individually

*DIVISION*  
*SUB-DIVISION*  
*CURRENCY*

*SCHEDULE P6*

*DATE*

*BUSINESS PLAN 19    /*  
*SUB-DIVISIONAL SUMMARY*

|  | | Actual | | | Original plan | Est. as at period | Plan | | |
|---|---|---|---|---|---|---|---|---|---|
| Year | 1 | 2 | 3 | 4 | 5 | 6 | 7 | 8 | 9 |
| Row no. | | | | | | | | | |
| Total sales external to subdivision   1 | | | | | | | | | |
| Trading profit HCA   2 | | | | | | | | | |
| Depreciation HCA   3 | | | | | | | | | |
| Depreciation CCA   4 | | | | | | | | | |
| Fixed capital expenditure   5 | | | | | | | | | |
| Trading cash flow   6 | | | | | | | | | |
| Fixed assets HCA   7 | | | | | | | | | |
| Fixed assets CCA   8 | | | | | | | | | |
| Working capital   9 | | | | | | | | | |
| Trading capital HCA   10 | | | | | | | | | |
| Trading capital CCA   11 | | | | | | | | | |
| *Ratios* Profit margin HCA   12 | | | | | | | | | |
| Working capital/sales   13 | | | | | | | | | |
| ROTC HCA   14 | | | | | | | | | |

*SCHEDULE P7*

*DIVISION*
*CURRENCY*

*DATE*
*BUSINESS PLAN 19    /*
*SALES AND PROFITS SUMMARY*

|  | Year | Actual | Original plan | Estimate as at period | | Plan | |
|---|---|---|---|---|---|---|---|
|  |  | 1 | 2 | 3 | 4 | 5 | 6 | 7 |
|  | Row no. | | | | | | | |
| Total divisional sales | 1 | | | | | | | |
| Inter-group sales | 2 | | | | | | | |
| Total external sales | 3 | | | | | | | |
| Trading profit | 4 | | | | | | | |
| Associated companies | 5 | | | | | | | |
| Operating profit | 6 | | | | | | | |
| Net interest group | 7 | | | | | | | |
| Net interest external | 8 | | | | | | | |
| Profit before tax | 9 | | | | | | | |
| Taxation: current | 10 | | | | | | | |
| Taxation: deferred | 11 | | | | | | | |
| Taxation: associates | 12 | | | | | | | |
| Profit after taxation | 13 | | | | | | | |
| Outside shareholders | 14 | | | | | | | |
| Attributable profit | 15 | | | | | | | |
| Extraordinary items | 16 | | | | | | | |
| Inter dividends | 17 | | | | | | | |
| Outside shareholders' dividends | 18 | | | | | | | |
| HCA retained profit | 19 | | | | | | | |

# Index